TRADITIONAL TEXTILES OF
CENTRAL ASIA

JANET HARVEY

TRADITIONAL TEXTILES OF
CENTRAL ASIA

With 262 illustrations, 212 in colour, and 2 maps

THAMES AND HUDSON

To Rupert and Melissa

Thanks to Janet Anderson, Tim and Feridith Ashfield, Bambi (friend of the late John, pioneer of Forbidden Fruit), Olivia Bristol, Mary E. Burkett, Elena Tsareva and Tatiana Emeljanenko of the Central Asian Department, Ethnologi Museum, St. Petersburg, for an insight into the museum's wonderful collection of textiles held in store, Peter and Elizabeth Collingwood, Joyce Doel, Jill Essery, Maria Fields, Phil Hague, Richard Harris and Sally Mathews, Inman Harvey, my father Raymond Hull, Dave and Maggie Kemp, Cynthia Kendzior, Rosie McMurray, Akbar Rakhimov, Tess Recordon, Nest Rubio, Montse Stanley, Noemi Speiser, Marsha Stanykovich and Sergai Mouraviev, Karun Thakar, John Pilkington, Ann Stevens for her 'magic pen', and the many people who afforded help and hospitality during my travels.

Special thanks for their time and loan of textiles to Pip Rau and Alastair Hull; and to John Gillow, without whose enthusiasm and knowledge on location this would be a lesser publication.

J.H.

Frontispiece
Suzani design, with the large medallion typical of hangings produced in the Bokhara area in the early period of the Uzbek Khanate.

Jacket illustration
Ceremonial tunic detail, textile loaned from the collection of Karun Thakar, The Rug Gallery, Leicester.

British Library Cataloguing-in-Publication Data
A catalogue record for this book is available from the British Library

ISBN 0-500-01670-4

Printed and bound in Hong Kong by Kwong Fat Offset Printing Co. Ltd.

Contents

Preface 6

Preface

The remote region at the heart of Asia had long held a fascination for me. Tales of great camel caravans crossing desert and high mountain pass to carry silk from China of the Han Dynasty to the markets of Imperial Rome; the romance of legendary mounted nomads who lived in felt-covered tents and who knew no boundaries or barriers; the history, sometimes terrible and sometimes glittering, evidence of which lies abandoned along the ancient trade routes, were all part of the dream to explore. But the reality was then a land closed to travellers. For four hundred years prior to 1991 when the political situation changed, a traveller's security which had once been provided by the Mongol rulers was no longer guaranteed; after their empire had fragmented in the fifteenth century the area was hostile to outsiders, and only the most intrepid ventured into Central Asia. During the same period internal discord caused many inhabitants to leave their homes and traditional pasturelands. Many fled the heartlands, taking with them the family's wealth in textiles, to join their tribal kinsfolk south of the River Oxus in Afghanistan. It was to Afghanistan, on the fringe of Central Asia, but inhabited by people integrated in the same history, that I travelled in the 1960s, and first encountered the extraordinary textiles of Central Asia.

The subtle shades of red and indigo of intricately woven rugs and bags, so intrinsic to the nomadic way of life; the brilliant colours of ikat-dyed silk robes, brought from the oasis towns; the floral designs of densely embroidered hangings and covers and the vivid patterns of nomad bodices and skirt-hem lengths were all displayed among the goods for sale in the streets and bazaars. I travelled widely, using local transport, along the bumpy tracks which are the ancient 'ways' of nomadic tribes. Occasionally a family would be on the move, the animals laden with woven bags and the women magnificent in their dresses. In nomad encampments the activity of producing the essential fabrics and furnishings was apparent at once in the warp pegged out on the ground, and piles of shorn fleece waiting to be made into felt or spun.

More recently, as the frontiers opened to the Central Asian region, it was possible to explore the oasis towns and mountain villages. Here the home-industry of sericulture is announced by small domed buildings used to rear silkworms and ancient plantations of mulberry trees. When I was welcomed into a house I found much of the living space taken up by a vertical loom where women weave beautiful traditional rugs and other necessities for the family and for sale.

Although the pace of social change has accelerated in the past decades, warps are still being pegged out on the desert ground, and women continue to gain status with their exquisite embroidery. I have no doubt that when I next return I shall again find a man from Hazarajat standing on a street corner selling from his barrow piled high with gloves, socks, pullovers and hats knitted by the people of his village.

The chapters which follow describe the wide range of the region's textile, from the historical fabrics to the unique and exquisite objects – made with limited means but with the knowledge of an ancient living tradition – to the products of more modern design and technology. Starting with the decorative motifs and the preparation of the materials, through dyeing, feltmaking, different weaving techniques and dress, to embroidery and block-printing, *Traditional Textiles of Central Asia* is an essential guide for the traveller, student, designer and collector.

(Top) Border of a wedding canopy, *bolim posh*, with floral discs and local legume-flowers.

1   The History and Motifs

The tribes of the Central Asian steppeland have made a significant mark on world history, yet documentation of the area could be considered neglected, and our knowledge to have advanced little beyond a romantic folklore, orally transmitted in the form of epic songs based on tales of the hunt, or mythical beasts, or strong charismatic leaders who banded together tribes and led them in rampages across the steppe. The nomadic life-style of the Central Asian tribes contributes to the fact that little remains in the form of archaeological or written record. Moreover, until the relatively recent discovery in Chinese archives of a collection of genealogies, legends and historical facts written in Mongol script ('The Secret History of the Mongols'), the early documentation of the area was made by scribes of the surrounding settled societies who refer to the nomadic tribes in derogatory terms – not surprisingly, for the agriculturists and urban-dwellers of northern China were the perennial victims of the steppe-dwellers' raids (the Great Wall was built to keep them out). Fortunately burials in extraordinary conditions, such as the extremely dry climate of the Desert of Lop at Lou-lan, or the permafrost of the Pazyryk tombs in the High Altai where the remains were entombed in stone, have preserved textiles and artefacts which are proof of the sophisticated culture and artistic achievement of the 'barbarian' tribes and their trading links with surrounding civilizations.

In prehistoric times two ethnically different peoples had gradually populated the area. Agrarian settlers of Indo-European race moved eastwards, establishing oasis settlements throughout Transoxiana and around the Tarim Basin where rivers from the surrounding Pamir, T'ien Shan and Kun Lun ranges made habitation possible. Simultaneously warring nomadic Turkic tribes moved westwards from the northern and eastern steppelands. These were peoples of many different Mongoloid groups, culturally and linguistically individual but with the economy of nomadic pastoralism in common.

The nomads and settled peoples

The domestication of the horse was the most significant of the steps that led to the nomadic tribes' success, but a variety of indigenous animals were domesticated and bred over the millennia to fulfil the nomads' needs. Sheep, goats, camels and cattle, including yak at high altitudes, gave fleece and hair for the textiles needed for protection from the harsh climate. Excavations show that the knowledge of felting fleece developed very early in the history of the nomad civilization, so that felt tent-coverings and furnishings such as floor-mats and blankets, and felt hats, capes and boots afforded some comfort. The spinning of hair, fleece and vegetable fibres was learned in Neolithic times or earlier, and provided yarn for the techniques of knitting, crochet and weaving.

A nomad's territory is in one sense boundless, but there is an established path linking a tribe's seasonal pastures, known as 'the Way'. The packing up and moving of the tribe along the path was, and still is, a twice-yearly ritual in which bags and animal-trappings decorated with beads, shells, buttons and metal discs, long wrapped cords and tassels all add to the colour and ceremony. Many of the motifs woven or embroidered in the decoration of bags and trappings are totems for identification of

(Below) Leather and felt cut-out saddle decorations, preserved in the Pazyryk tombs, fourth century BC.

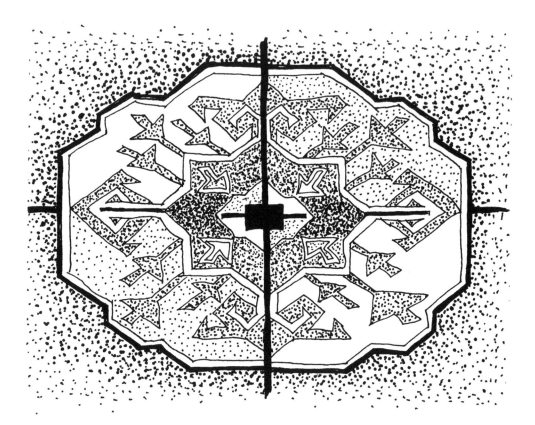

the tribe or group. The textiles themselves have evolved of necessity as portable storage vessels and furnishings, and the woven ropes and bands have a multiplicity of uses in the nomadic way of life, their fineness a measure of the wealth and prosperity of the tribe.

Turkmen tribal göl, *the emblem woven into rugs, bags and tent-bands.*

After centuries of animosity, the warring nomadic tribes and the settled agrarian population gradually learned that it was to their mutual advantage to live in harmony, and the town bazaar became the centre for the exchange of wares necessary to both societies.

Trade routes

Central Asia, at the heart of the landmass of Asia, extends from the Danube to the Pacific shores, bordered on the north by the forested *taiga* and to the south by high plateaux running from the Balkans to Tibet and the Chinese plains. This immense area has had contradictory roles in history, both separating the great civilizations on the periphery and connecting them with a network of overland trade routes, which at their zenith, from the end of the first millennium BC to the fourth century AD, carried luxury goods including silk, gems and spices to the West, and fine muslins, woollens and glass from India and Europe to China. The foreign influences carried along the routes left their permanent marks on the evolving culture of Central Asia, which had previously been shaped by purely local conditions.

The main route westward for great trade caravans out of China was first opened up by the Emperor Wu-ti (145-87 BC) who ruled the civilized, self-contained China of the Han Dynasty. Emperor Wu-ti had two vital concerns: the first the security of his empire, which was constantly raided by the Hsiung-nu from the north – the mounted nomads who four centuries later, when known as the Huns, brought devastation to the Roman Empire; the second, his own immortality. When he heard from his ambassador, Chang-ch'ien, of the horses that were kept by the Yueh-chih of the Ferghana valley – fine, swift horses, very different from the sturdy, stoical beasts indigenous to China – he decided that acquisition of these 'celestial horses' would be the answer to his problems, both as mounts for his cavalry and as a 'magical vehicle' to carry him to eternal happiness at the appropriate time. His request to the King of Ferghana for a few brood mares and a stallion was refused, and the mission returned sorely depleted by the rigours of the desert journey. Emperor Wu-ti was not to be defeated. He gathered together a great army, including engineers to divert rivers, and horticulturists to plant alfalfa for the horses, and sent them through some of the most hostile territory on earth on a three-thousand-mile round trip to Ferghana. A herd of steeds was finally brought back, and so was inaugurated the trail from China to the West which would develop in time into the well-trodden and celebrated trade route known today as the Silk Road.

With China's control over the Tarim Basin established, there began a period of rapidly increasing trade. Affluent Roman citizens had discovered an insatiable desire for the most luxurious of all fabrics – silk, which had already been produced in China, around the centre of Ch'ang An, for more than two thousand years. Thriving communities grew up in the oases around the Tarim Basin. Settlements such as Lou-lan, Charchan and Niya, when explored by Sir Aurel Stein in the early years of the twentieth century, 'yielded a rich antiquarian haul in quite bewildering confusion'. Clearing an ancient graveyard buried by sand, Stein found 'above all a wonderful variety of fabrics which delighted my eyes. Among them were pieces of beautifully coloured figured silks, fragments of rich tapestry work and embroidery as well as of pile carpets, by the side of coarse fabrics in wool and felt. It soon became evident that remnants of garments of all sorts had been used here as wrapping for bodies. I could not have wished for a more representative exhibition of that ancient silk trade which had been a chief factor in opening up this earliest route for China's direct intercourses with Central Asia and the distant west.'

The Turkmen tribes took full advantage of the opportunities for lucrative employment offered by the great caravans, and knew the routes and the perils of travelling through the hostile terrain of marshy swamps, shifting desert dunes driven by the hot summer wind, the *shamal*, or the bitter winter wind, the *bural*, the high mountain passes and endless empty steppe. They knew where to find the *saksaul* for fuel, the smooth pebble which carried in the mouth would stave off thirst, the deep bell-note of the lead camel and the high ring of the small bell on the last camel of the caravan.

Loads were taxed and bought and sold along the way by a new class of affluent merchants, who acted as middlemen for the goods in transit and distributed many new products to the local bazaars. Oases such as Khotan, Kashgar, Balkh and Merv expanded as centres of commerce, while Balkh became a hub of the trade routes, from which goods from the east went north to the towns of Bokhara and Samarkand and to settlements in the Ferghana Valley, or south through the passes of the Hindu Kush to Afghanistan and India, or westward, either through Persia to the Mediterranean countries or across the Caspian Sea and up the great rivers to Russia and the north. The town of Derbent on the west coast of the Caspian was, and still is, a renowned carpet-trading centre. Much merchandise changed hands at the 'Stone Tower,' thought to be the present-day Tashkurghan on the edge of the Pamir range, then the most easterly point of the Parthian Empire. The western world had no direct knowledge of the fabled land of Serinda (China), and traders were fearful of venturing too far into the unknown. In AD 41-54, Pliny recorded that goods carried to the Pamir 'are deposited on the further side of a certain river alongside those the Seres offer for sale, and the latter, if content with the bargain, carry them off'.

Over the centuries there were considerable fluctuations in the volume of East-West trade, with swings between the use of land routes and seaways according to the economic and political fortunes of the countries involved. Such fluctuations in turn determined the affluence of the cities, towns and settlements throughout Central Asia.

Commerce between the East and medieval Europe was dominated by the Italian city states, particularly Venice and Genoa, with a lengthy conduit for goods that

Map of the eastern and western regions of Central Asia (boxed areas), showing the oasis towns and the ancient trade routes that cross the region and radiate to the surrounding civilizations.

included camel caravan, Mediterranean shipping, and a host of voracious middlemen. Although valuable commodities such as spices and silk ensured that the trade remained worthwhile, the land routes became increasingly costly and dangerous with the rise of the Islamic Ottoman Empire and the growing hostility to Christian commerce via the Middle East. The desire to maintain trade links prompted maritime exploration. In 1498, sponsored by Prince Henry of Portugal, Vasco da Gama rounded the Cape of Good Hope into the Indian Ocean and landed on the Malabar Coast of India, thus opening up the maritime route to the East, with detrimental effect on the activity along the overland trade routes. By the beginning of the seventeenth century the expansion of maritime trade with the Far East and India had brought about the decline of the Central Asian towns reliant upon the great trade caravans, moving at camel-pace across the vast, empty terrain.

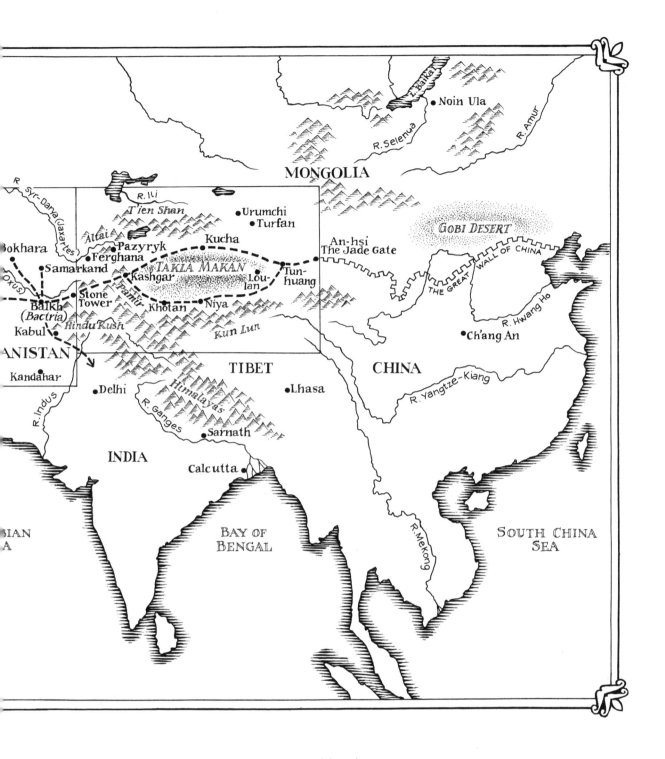

Jenghiz Khan and his legacy

Over the centuries a succession of tribes – among them the Sakas, the Scythians, the Sarmatians and Uighurs – rose, spread in waves, and then subsided in importance in the tribal hierarchy. Eventually, at the beginning of the thirteenth century, Turko-Mongolian tribes united under the leadership of the Mongol ruler Jenghiz Khan gained control of the whole region, creating an empire that extended from the Carpathian mountains to the Sea of Japan – the largest area ever to be dominated by a single dynasty. Upon the death of Jenghiz, in accordance with Mongol tradition, the empire was divided among his sons. The eastern region, the ancestral 'yurt', remained under the rule of the Great Khan, his direct successor, while the remainder of the territory was divided into three principal Khanates. The western territory, consisting of the vast steppe stretching from the River Selenga 'as far as the limits reached by the hooves of

11

stallions', was allotted to his son Juchi. In that age of warriors and war-lords, when unrelated tribal peoples were banded together under the rule of a chieftain they adopted his name as a sign of their political allegiance. A descendant of Juchi, Uzbek Khan (1312-1340), who ruled over the territory of the Golden Horde, was converted to Islam, and persuaded his subjects, the Uzbeks, to embrace the Muslim faith. Under his descendants, for two centuries, a unique Islamic culture developed among the nomad tribes, giving rise to the textiles and motifs so outstanding in Uzbek crafts today.

Towards the end of the fifteenth century an Uzbek army conquered much of Transoxiana, merged with the settled population, and gave rise to a dominant group in today's Central Asia, some sections of which live settled and some nomadic lives. The Lakai are a non-Muslim group who have separated themselves from the main body of the Uzbek, and maintain the tradition of mounted warrior-herdsmen of the steppe long after other tribes have abandoned this life-style. The symbols of their vibrant free-style embroidery reflect their ancient way of life, with the association of sun- and fire-worship in the circular motifs.

During the five centuries following the decline of the Chinese Han Dynasty the trade caravans had been constantly subject to bandit attack, until in the early thirteenth century the conquests of Jenghiz Khan inaugurated a period of efficient administration under the Mongol Khanates, and the fullest encouragement was offered to merchants and every aspect of trade. Currency was standardized throughout the landways, and military post-stations, established at regular intervals along the routes, enforced the law and provided accommodation for caravans. It is recorded that at this time 'a maiden bearing a nugget of gold could safely wander the realm'. Travellers

Traditional women's dress of a Kirghiz nomad family.

Tent of a Buddhist teacher, richly furnished with silk-brocade and appliqué felt. Buddhism was established in the region between the fifth and ninth centuries, and the rich endowment of monasteries permitted the production of fine textiles.

from the West, among them the Venetian merchant Marco Polo, and the Friars Carpini and William of Rubruck who were sent with dispatches from the Pope to the Great Khan, left vivid records of their travels, remarking upon the barbarian nomads living in their felt-covered tents.

The cultural development of the urban settlements of Central Asia reached its zenith between the mid-fourteenth century and the end of the sixteenth century, during the period of the Timurid Empire. Timur was a descendant of a commander of Jenghiz Khan's army who established a sub-tribe in Transoxiana and rose to power during the time of decline of the Mongol Empire, owing his remarkable success as an empire-builder to his ability to embrace the values of both nomad and settled populations. His conquest in the Islamic domain of Persia and Arabia opened the way for the establishment of Islamic faith, art and culture in all parts of Central Asia. Thousands of craftsmen, the captives of his campaigns, were brought to the cities of his homeland, Samarkand, Bokhara and Herat, to practise their skills as builders, potters, metalworkers, calligraphers, printers, bookbinders, weavers and embroiderers. Samarkand emerged as a magnificent capital city where the feudal system enabled the ruling families to acquire enormous wealth, and patronage of craft workshops encouraged the production of exquisite textiles. Trade was fostered throughout the Empire, and caravans thronged the routes between East and West.

Craft guilds were established and textile workshops continued to flourish until the nineteenth century, providing exquisite *abr* (ikat) silks, opulent gold-thread and silk embroidery and fine cotton weaves. Woven and printed cotton cloth from the Bokhara district was particularly appreciated for its beauty; export to Persia and India had been

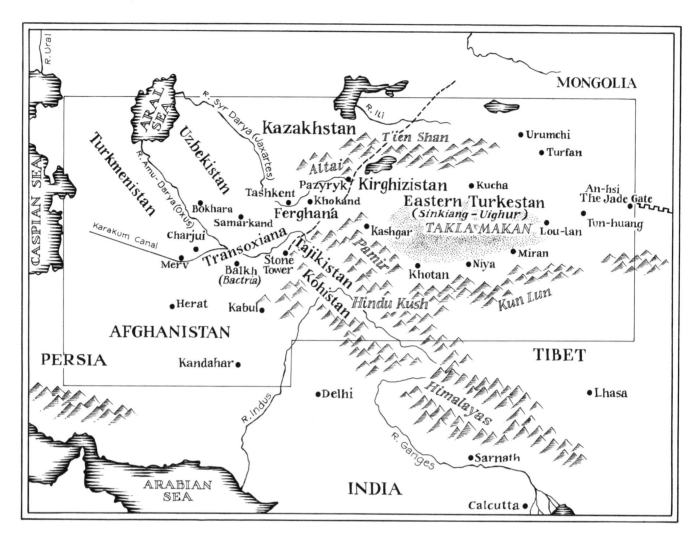

documented in the tenth century, and until the nineteenth century it remained an important item of export to Russia.

Rural Central Asia today retains the legacy of the Mongol campaigns of the thirteenth and fourteenth centuries in a population of tribal groups, each of whom takes pride in their identity. Two such are the Kirghiz and Kazakh, who follow the age-old nomadic way of life, herding their flocks in the Pamir and T'ien Shan mountains and selling their surplus wool in the bazaars of the local settlements. They live in felt-covered tents and embellish their bags, floor-coverings and furnishings with embroidery. A smaller group of Mongol origin living within a Tadjik population is descended from the thousand-strong garrison posted by Jenghiz Khan to guard conquered mountain territory in central Afghanistan. Known as the Hazara ('one thousand'), they are renowned for their fine-patterned Fair Isle type of knitting and chain-stitch embroidery.

West of the Pamir barrier the population consists of an ethnic mix of Tadjiks, the original Persian-speaking settlers and Turkmen, Uzbek and other Turkic tribespeople who have taken up a settled life-style and are known as Sarts, together with communities of Jewish settlers and other groups who came to the area as traders or missionaries, or sometimes as refugees or captives. In Eastern Turkestan the Han Chinese have had more cultural influence, although the Uighur, a Turkic nomadic tribe who settled, developed an alphabetic script and became administrators of the Mongol Empire, now dominate Kashgar and towns on the northern rim of the Tarim. Khotan and southern Chinese Turkestan received groups of traders from Taxila in North India in the first century AD, and the descendants of these still are evident today, while groups of Tibetan origin are settled in Khotan and towns in the south.

Tribal areas of Central Asia. The dotted line marks the 'friendship border' agreed between the USSR and China, dividing tribal grazing-pastures.

(Opposite) Interior of a Kirghiz tent in the Pamirs, with textiles piled around the lattice walls.

Textiles since the Khanates

During the sixteenth century a series of tribal civil wars had led to the decline in the power of the nomadic tribes, and the establishment of the Uzbek aristocracy. Disunity throughout Central Asia encouraged the advance of Russia under the rule of Peter I, eager to exploit the Central Asian routes to India and to secure the land-border against British intrusion from the south, through Afghanistan and over the mountain passes of the Hindu Kush and the Pamirs. The Chinese-Russian border was first established with the signing of the Treaty of Nerchinsk in August 1689. Since then there have been many adjustments, based on such transient factors as the line of nomad pasture pickets. In 1950 the two great powers finally agreed the present 'friendship border' which cuts through Central Asia in a broad sweep from the Pamir heights to the Pacific coast. Many tribal groups have been, and still are, divided by the borderline, and must accept a dual hegemony.

When in the nineteenth century the powerful Khanates fell, not without a struggle, into the hands of the Bolsheviks, the production of luxury textiles which had flourished since the Timurid period came to an abrupt halt. Russian administrators took the place of the court hierarchy, and textile production was reorganized into large, mechanized State-run factories. The importation of cotton yarn from the rapidly expanding Russian spinning-factories and the use of imported synthetic dyes noticeably altered the character of Central Asian woven and printed cloth. To meet the demands of the Russian market, weavers developed new patterns in brighter colours, or severe, graphic designs with two or three colour-contrasts, in place of the traditional subtle polychromy. However, during the 1960s a growing interest in national crafts prompted a revival of the age-old techniques of small-scale textile manufacture.

Entertainers of the oasis towns, dressed in flamboyant ikat robes.

After the 1917 revolution both townspeople and nomad tribes fled the area; but in recent times, with the new turn of the political wheel, many descendants of those who took refuge south of the River Oxus have fled once again to escape the Russian invasion of Afghanistan. Commercial enterprises utilizing the traditional techniques of Central Asia have been established in neighbouring countries to produce embroideries and weavings for export.

While the nomadic population of Central Asia diminishes in numbers, and the settled population has no further need of the panniers and covers, bands and ropes indispensable on migration, the tradition of weaving and embroidery remains deeply ingrained. Many homes contain a loom where women weave articles for domestic use or for sale in the bazaar: rugs and bags, chair-covers for the home or seat-covers for the car, saddle-covers for the horse or the bicycle. Only the desire for beautiful dowry textiles has diminished with the cultural changes. The superb *suzanis,* bags and carpets, woven and stitched with love and pride to adorn the new home and honour its guests, are now seldom seen.

1 (Opposite) Large felt floor-covering, *numdah.* Some of the cut-out shapes for the pattern are stitched to the felt backing while others are felted-in.

2 (Left) Uzbek wallhanging or platform-cover (detail). The motifs are the tribal emblems, *göl*, worked in silk thread on plain-woven wool cloth dyed a subtle shade of madder-red.

3 (Above) Uzbek *ghudjeri*, an all-purpose cover made from narrow warp-face patterned bands, cut to length and joined at the selvedges. The simplicity of the tribeswomen's looms limits the weaving of wider patterned pieces.

4 Large embroidered wallhanging, *suzani*, worked with a tambour hook in thick silk-twist on cotton. The motifs of floral discs and pomegranate-flowers, with Islamic influence in the trellis-pattern, suggest it was worked for an urban girl's dowry in the Bokhara area.

5 (Right) Detail of a nineteenth-century bed-cover, *adiol*. To make the complex *abr* pattern the silk warp-threads were bound and dyed at least six times.

6-8 Portable textile furnishings are necessary in nomad life. (Left) Hazara storage-bag, *juval*, designed to hang on the tent trellis-wall, or be carried on the camel's side when the tribe is on the move.

(Below) Balouch Malaki *juval*, with intricate weft-faced pattern further enriched with tassels and cords, shells and blue-glass beads.

(Bottom) Patterned bed-quilts lining a Kirghiz nomad-family's tent.

9-10 (Above) Kirghiz felt-covered tent or yurt, the door-flap patterned with felt appliqué. (Above right) Caravan of camels laden with the goods and chattels of a nomadic tribe.

11 (Below) Free-wheeling floral discs embroidered in silk-thread tambour on an Uzbek Lakai padded-cotton saddle-cover.

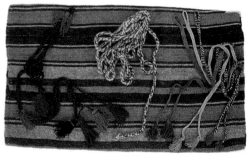

12-13 Trappings of nomadic life.
(Left) Detail of woven tent-bands, *iolam*.
Over 12 metres (40 ft) long, these girths
for the tent-walls display the tribal
emblems, *göl*.

14-17 (Top) Camel head-harness and
knee-pads, rich with braids, crown
knots, tassels, pearl buttons, beads and
shells. (Centre) Turkmen *okbash*, a pair
of bags to cover the ends of the tent-roof
struts when in transit.(Above) Braided
ropes and a strong striped woollen sack,
with many uses in the nomad way
of life.

18 Ersari Turkmen *jallar*, storage-bag, one of a particularly fine pair made to hang at either side of a camel. The knotted-pile face displays the tribal göl.

19 (Left) The solar disc motif inherited from the ancient sun cult of the region, embellishing a Lakai *lali posh*, food-cover.

20 (Below) Sun-disc motif, rooted in ancient beliefs, and a border design inspired by legume-plants indigenous to the area, decorating a *bolim posh*, the canopy held over the bride and groom during the wedding ceremony, from Urgut, near Samarkand.

21 Solar discs entwined with arabesques derived from Islamic pattern, exquisitely embroidered on a *suzani* hanging from Shakhrisabz, near Samarkand.

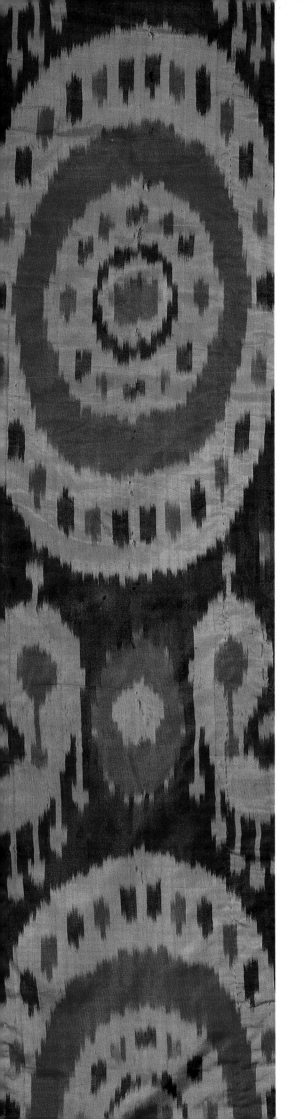

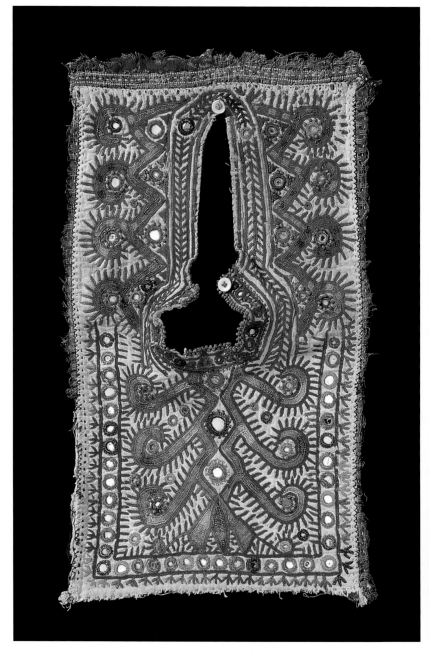

22-4 Traditional motifs appear in the designs of sophisticated urban silks, no less than in the patterns embroidered by village and nomad women. Discs (far left) dominating the design of *abr* silk. (Left) Stars charmingly decorating a felt Kirghiz camel-flank trapping, *asamlyk*. (Below left) The tree of life inset with *shisha* mirrors to deflect the evil eye, stitched on a Hazara girl's dress-front.

25-7 (This page) The tree of life (above), symbolic of the levels of the universe, embroidered in satin and chain stitch on the back of a Pashtun nomad man's homespun cotton tunic. (Below) Solar disc, star motifs and trees of life, worked in satin stitch edged with white beads on a Kohistani woman's shawl. (Right) The tree of life patterning *abr* silk.

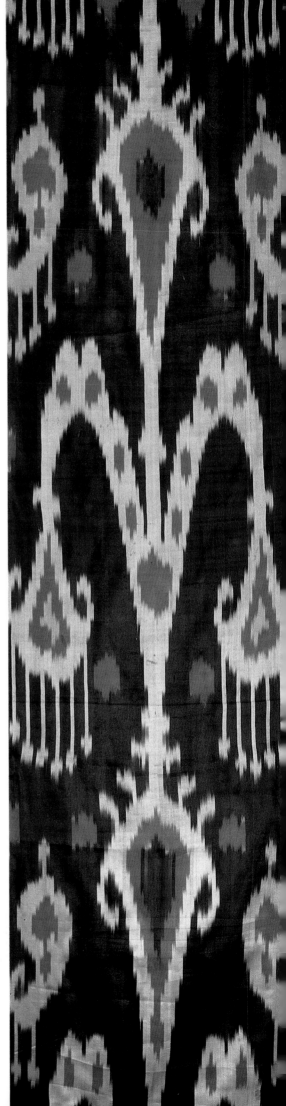

28-31 Motifs are sometimes credited with powers of 'sympathetic magic'. Hunting cloths made around Herat (above and below) are stencilled, painted and block-printed with real and mythical beasts, to be hung on bushes or in lodges to appease the spirit of the hunted animal. Scorpions (right) embroidered on a pair of long woollen puttees are believed to protect the legs of the wearer from the live insect.

32 (Opposite) Scorpion motifs among the zigzags of an ikat-dyed silk hanging, *pardah*, from the Ferghana region.

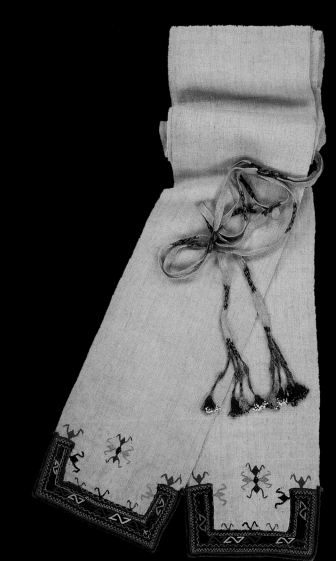

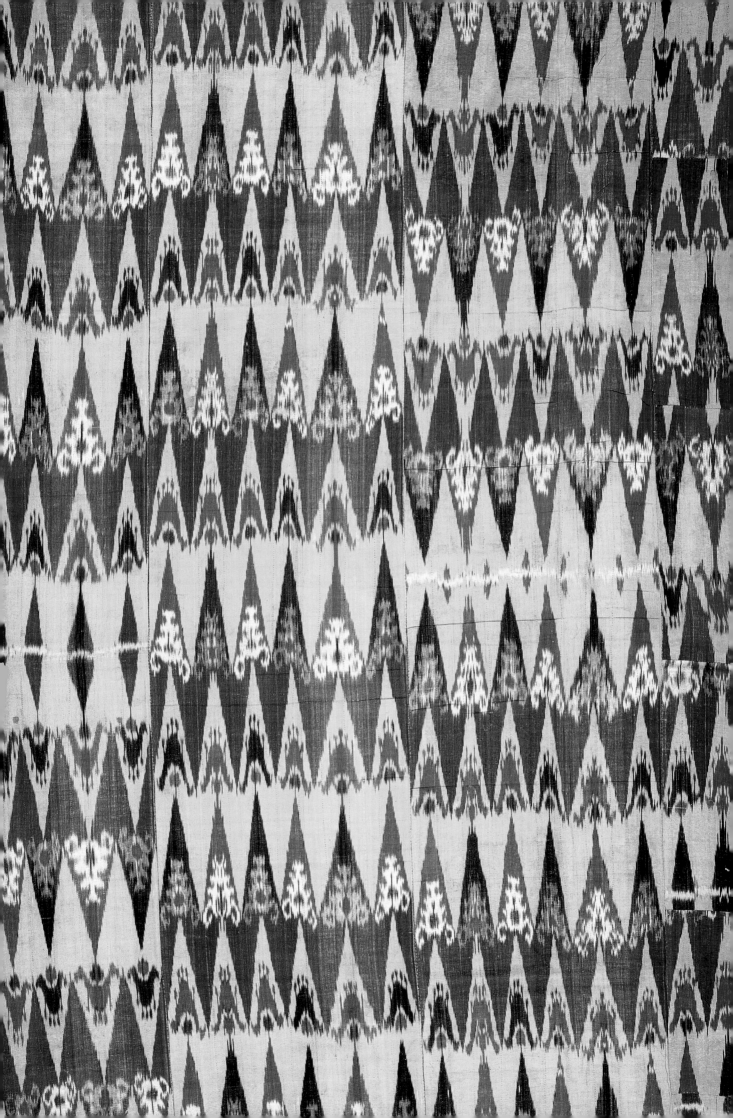

33 Cover for the nuptial bed, *ruidigo*, stitched for a dowry in the Bokhara area.
Carnations and pomegranate-flowers are symbols of fruitfulness, beautifully worked in
silk-thread tambour.

34 The ram's horn motif, an ancient emblem of success and strength in the hunt, outlined in bold yellow chain stitch on a Lakai woman's mirror-bag.

35 The tulip, of all Central Asian flowers the one most vividly evoking springtime and blossoming, embroidered on a Tekke tribeswoman's gown, *chyrpy*. The colour – yellow – denotes the woman's married status.

36 (Left) Pomegranate-flowers suspended from ram's horns, motifs signifying strength and abundance, woven into a man's ikat-dyed coat, *chapan*.

37 The Islamic motif of the *mihrab* (arch) with a stylized version of the older, Buddhist-derived trailing-lotus motif, embroidered on a cotton *djoinamoz*, a cloth for use as a prayer mat or wallhanging.

38 The *mihrab* motif (below), flanked by the stylized hands of a legendary local figure, combined with the tree of life and stars, embroidered on a cotton cloth to wrap the *mohr*, a holy stone used in Muslim worship, from Hazarajat.

39 (Facing page) New motifs sometimes enter a design through the embroiderer's or weaver's wish to incorporate some striking image from their own lives. So a Turkmen knotted-pile prayer rug from Afghanistan includes a helicopter gunship among the camels and flowers in the *mihrab*.

40-44 Embroidery is considered a protective element in its own right. Worked round garment-openings like sleeves and pockets, it guards the wearer from harmful forces. (Top) Antlered animals and flowers edging the cuffs of a Tekke Turkmen *chyrpy*. (Above) *Shisha* mirrors to avert evil, embroidered on the cuffs of a shirt from Hazarajat. (Above right) Embroidered ankle-bands. (Right) Floral discs on the band joining a *chyrpy*'s vestigial sleeves. (Below) Lacing stitch (*kesdi*) densely worked at the neck of a Mangelli nomad's tunic.

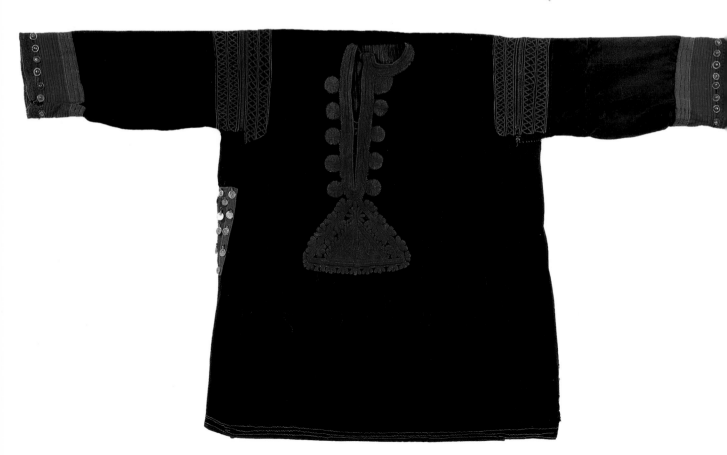

45 Hooked disc motifs to guard the hem and side-slits of a Turkmen robe, worked in lacing stitch (*kesdi*) and chain stitch.

46 (Below) Infants and young children are protected from misfortune in a variety of ways. A Turkmen child's ceremonial tunic is heavily laden with amulets, including coins, discs, bells, blue beads, cowrie-shells, and a small silver box, complete with horns, to hold a text from the Koran.

47 Long embroidered extensions on the backs of the skull-caps of Kirghiz women, designed to safeguard the vulnerable nape of the neck and plait of hair.

48 (Below) Cover for the neck and back of the camel that carries a Tekke Turkmen bride to her wedding, made predominantly in the life-giving colour red, and stitched with tufts of a child's hair, visible on the centre panel.

49-54 The most common form of the amulet, the triangle. It may be embroidered with gold thread (far left) to be stitched on to clothing, or decorated in cross stitch as a small pouch to hold a text from the Koran (left), or beaded and embroidered (left below) to fix to clothing, bags or trappings.

55-7 (Below) Kohistani children's hats, worn constantly in the harsh mountain climate, and elaborately worked with protective motifs and amulets. Embroidered ear-flaps and long back panels safeguard the most vulnerable areas of the head.

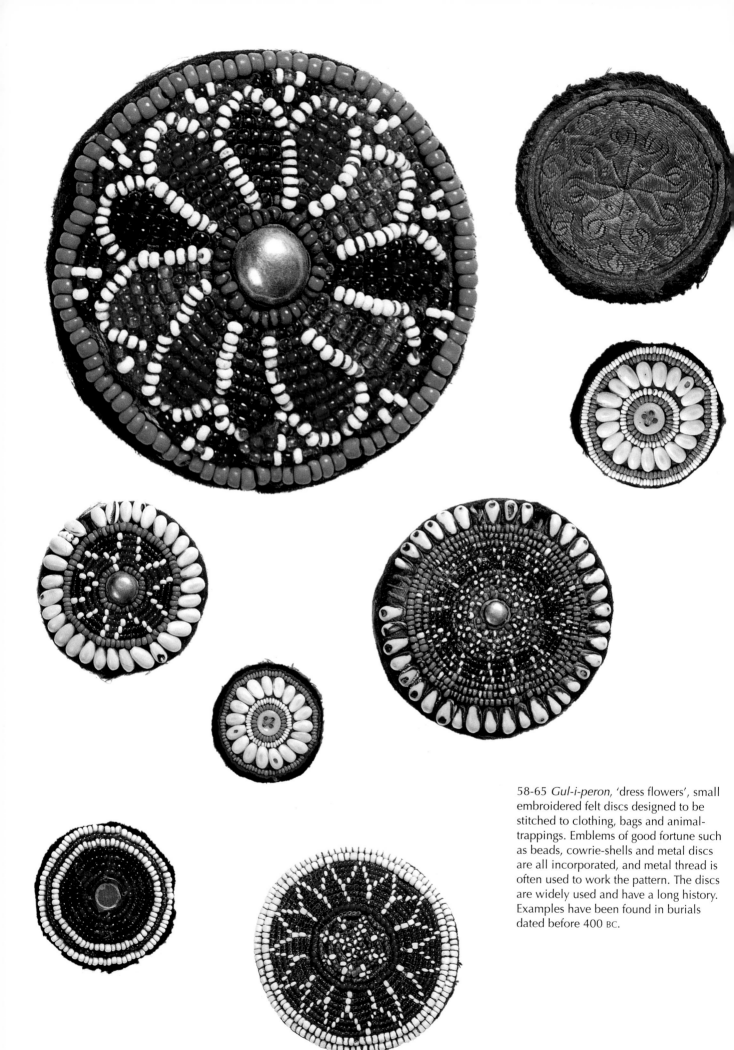

58-65 *Gul-i-peron*, 'dress flowers', small embroidered felt discs designed to be stitched to clothing, bags and animal-trappings. Emblems of good fortune such as beads, cowrie-shells and metal discs are all incorporated, and metal thread is often used to work the pattern. The discs are widely used and have a long history. Examples have been found in burials dated before 400 BC.

The Decorative Motifs

Inherited from the practise of shamanism of the earliest inhabitants of Central Asia is the belief in the life-giving or threatening forces of nature which require constant appeasement. Woven or embroidered images may communicate a belief or an aspiration, express a fear or represent an offering. Symbolic motifs decorate clothing and every other type of felt and woven textile. Where once a soothsayer would pour a drop of oil on to the surface of a bowl of water (symbolic of a family's living enclave, the *yurt*) and watch the swirling spread of oil, reading omens in the patterns, so today artists will watch the oil for inspiration when they bind the silk warp used to weave the *abr* cloth. Hunters use animals depicted on cloths to hang in the lodge or on bushes; or the image of a harmful animal or insect, such as the scorpion, is embroidered on a textile to protect the wearer from the live creature.

Motifs take a variety of forms according to the craft-technique employed. The grid-structure of weaving or counted-thread embroidery, for instance, is reflected in stylized geometric motifs, whereas felt decoration or chain-stitch embroidery gives rise to a naturalistic or free-flowing type of design. So a star may appear as a solid five-, six- or eight-pointed figure on an embroidered or *sumach*-woven textile, but be stylized into an arrangement of triangles on a kelim-woven rug.

Foreign influences

The establishment of the trade routes between East and West and southwards to the Indian sub-continent brought many non-indigenous motifs to be integrated with traditional Central Asian patterns. Motifs of steppeland flowers, for example, became 'bunched' in emulation of the Persian *butah* motif, seen on weavings and embroidery brought to Transoxiana when Cyrus expanded the Achaemenian kingdom in the fifth century BC. With the knowledge of the drawloom came the ability to produce complicated repeat patterns, such as the Persian motif of a roundel containing birds or beasts, or the tree of life. Although not widely used in Central Asian domestic weaving, the roundel or medallion motif became fashionable in urban weaving workshops. The urban inhabitants of Central Asia were well versed in Western techniques and styles by the time Alexander the Great, after defeating Darius III in 330 BC, conquered the whole Persian Empire, with the territory as far as the River Jaxartes and south through Afghanistan into India. Following his policy to integrate with the conquered peoples, he married Roxane, the beautiful daughter of a chieftain of northern Afghanistan. Many boys in this area are to this day named Iskandar, the Persian version of Alexander, while the Greek artistic legacy is evident in the clear lines of Greek classical art blended with Indian Buddhist forms in motifs of the unique Gandharan style, found in northern Afghanistan and throughout the Bactrian plains.

Star motif on a kelim-woven rug (right), and on a *sumach*-woven bag (far right).

Horn or antler motif, woven in weft-face patterning on a Balouch grain-sack.

After the death of Alexander and the division of the kingdom among his generals, one, Seleucus, maintained the influence of Hellenistic culture over the Bactrian plains and the Hindu Kush. Excavation of royal graves at Ay Khanoum and Tillya Tepe brought to light clothing in a combination of Greek and Mongolian style, ornamented with gold discs bearing Greek and Archaemenid designs as well as indigenous Scythian motifs of entwined animal forms.

During the first half of the first century AD waves of invading nomadic tribes pushed southwards over Bactria, through Afghanistan and into north-west India. First came the Parthians, who brought to this southern area the vigorous zoomorphic forms characteristic of Scythian art. They were followed by the aggressive Kushan tribe who established an empire through Gandhara as far as the River Ganges, converted to Buddhism and thus opened a route for the religion to enter Central Asia and thence be carried to China. Agrarian fertility deities and ferocious shamanic gods found a place in the Buddhist pantheon as protectors, and Buddhist motifs of the endless thread of fortune, the lotus and the mandala became interspersed with Central Asian sun symbols, moons or horned motifs. From the fifth to ninth centuries rich endowment of Buddhist monasteries permitted the production of fine woven-silk brocades and painted silk *tankas*.

The urban-dwellers of Central Asia embraced Islam during the seventh and eighth centuries as the faith was carried eastwards along the trade routes from the sources of Mecca and Medina in Arabia, gradually spreading outward to reach the nomadic population. Even remote areas in the valleys of the Hindu Kush, where ancient animistic beliefs were maintained until the late nineteenth century, were finally converted to Islam under pressure from the British administration of the North-West Frontier. Kafiristan, the land of unbelievers, became Nuristan, the land of light.

Islamic pattern incorporates free-flowing floral arabesque and calligraphy into disciplined, mathematically inspired, geometric self-generating designs – a language of order and unity. Symbolic shapes connected with Muslim beliefs, such as the *mihrab* (arch), and the hand of Fatima, were combined with the traditional patterns of Central Asian textiles.

Islamic worship is devoid of ritual items apart from the prayer mat, *namazlyk*. Muslim households and mosques possess many mats made in every technique – felted, flat-woven or knotted pile, embroidered or printed. Generally the 'field' of the mat is the *mihrab*, with a symmetrical border infilled with a multitude of traditional

Vigorous composition of a horned ram and tiger in the Animal Style of ancient Scythian art. Cut-out of leather ornamenting a saddle-cover found in the Pazyryk tombs, fourth century BC.

Hooked sun-disc (right), worked in chain stitch on a Lakai saddle-cover.

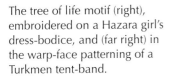

The tree of life motif (right), embroidered on a Hazara girl's dress-bodice, and (far right) in the warp-face patterning of a Turkmen tent-band.

motifs, including tribal emblems (*göl*), the tree of life, rams' horns and stars. A vital item of popular belief is the amulet, and an Islamic form found throughout Central Asia consists of words of the Koran inscribed on paper and encased in a triangle of embroidered cloth worn stitched on clothing, animal-trappings, bags, or even the cap.

Traditional motifs and their significance

The majority of textiles are, and always have been, made by women, who thereby become the custodians of the visual expression of their tribe or group. Prior to the radical social changes of the early twentieth century, the motifs and patterns of felts, weavings and embroideries retained a strong traditional element, displaying symbols of great antiquity side by side with more recent Graeco-Roman, Buddhist or Islamic patterns and images. The Animal Style of the Scythian tribes, with a vigorous interplay of zoomorphic forms, is rooted in shamanism, and decorates the earliest textiles discovered in Central Asia, from the burial sites of Pazyryk and Noin Ula. Natural forms such as flowers, stars, or an article from everyday home-life may suggest the wish of a weaver or embroiderer to put into the work some meaningful element of her environment. Nowadays, for example, the weapons of war which have dominated the lives of those living in Afghanistan over the past decade are incorporated into weavings and embroideries, demonstrating just such an impulse.

While interpretation of motifs in textile decoration must always be speculative, since meanings change with the cultural context, a variety of motifs have broadly similar symbolic connotations wherever they are applied.

The bird, a common motif, is understood to mediate between this world and the world of the spirits. The cock, usually stylized as a head and comb (p. 119), represents the harbinger of the day which dispels the spirits of darkness. Birds of prey, during the medieval period totems of some of the Turkic tribes, are the emblems of power and nobility, especially when double-headed.

The tree of life, the *axis mundi*, ascends through the three spheres, the roots springing from the underworld, the trunk rising through the terrestrial world and the branches piercing the heavens. The tree's seasonal cycle is associated symbolically with the universal cycle of birth, maturity, death and rebirth.

Horned and antlered animals were of vital importance to the lives of the primitive hunters who became the nomadic pastoralists of Central Asia. The dangers of the hunt and its successful conclusion were assured by rituals involving a head of antlers or horns which magically endowed the shaman with the spirit of the hunted creature. Many stylized textile motifs are based on curved horns or branched antlers.

The ancient cult of worship of the sun and fire as life-giving forces was widespread in the region, and gave rise to a variety of motifs such as solar discs and swastikas, which represent the revolution of the sun, as well as the allied star and moon motifs.

For the survival of any pastoral society the fertility of humans and animals is a foremost concern. The pomegranate with its abundance of seeds features on the embroidered marriage-bed cover, *ruidigo*, and on *suzani*, the embroidered squares which hang as curtains round the bed. Locks of a child's hair are stitched on to a camel-trapping for the wedding procession. Cowrie shells, associated with female fertility, and the small conch-shell with its spiral interior, also used in rain-bringing ritual, are incorporated among the tassels and decoration of woven bags used for storing domestic utensils.

A flower of particular significance in Central Asia as a sign of the coming of spring – the season known as *eulnek*, 'the blossoming of the fields' – is the tulip, which blooms so abundantly when the snow-melt brings moisture to the dusty steppelands. Babur, the ousted chieftain of Central Asia who became the first Mogul emperor of India, was a literate man and a lover of nature who kept a meticulous diary of his observations. In this he identifies sixteen different varieties of tulip in the hills around Kabul. As a decorative motif the tulip is symbolic of abundance and fertility, and it is frequently embroidered on the Turkmen woman's gown or *chyrpy*, and on *suzani*. Stylized tulip-forms also decorate knotted-pile and woven textiles, and knitting.

As tribal identities developed a particular motif would be adopted as the tribal emblem, or *göl*. *Göl* are usually octagonal or diamond-shaped medallions with complex infilling of symmetrical patterns. A conquered tribe would be obliged to incorporate the *göl* of the tribe to whom it owed allegiance into its main weavings,

Göl of a Turkmen tribe (right).

Fertility symbols of carnations and pomegranate-flowers (top left), embroidered on a nuptial bed-cover, *ruidigo,* and the tulip motif (left) embroidered on Turkmen woman's *chyrpy.*

Beadwork triangular amulet (below).

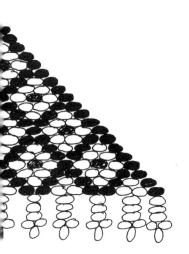

usually the rugs and carpets for the tent, while its own *göl* would be relegated to the borders or to smaller articles such as tent-bands. Sixty or so different motifs might be woven into one tent-band, including tribal *göls* and named symbolic patterns, such as *buynuz,* the horn motif, *ok gozi,* the arrow-point motif, or *yulduz,* the star motif.

People of all faiths, Muslim, Buddhist or Nestorian Christian, no less than those with deep-rooted animistic beliefs, share the concept of the amulet which safeguards the wearer or household. Charms take many different forms, but the triangle is the most common. Made of felt, it is hung over the doorway of the *yurt.* Woven, embroidered or knotted, it makes the twin flank-trappings of the wedding camel. Small embroidered or beadwork triangles are stitched on to the clothing.

Decorative embroidery is also used as a protective element in itself. Often forming symbolic patterns, it is worked round the edges and openings of garments – hems, pockets, necklines – through which harmful forces are likely to attack the body. Vulnerable areas – especially the front bodice, the head and nape of the neck – are dressed in heavy embroidery. Shiny objects such as coins, metal discs, or in the south of the area, mirrors (*shisha*), incorporated in the embroidery are believed to avert the evil eye, or reflect and hold its image thus absorbing the destructive powers. Blue beads are similarly sewn on or woven or braided into fabric as a protective device.

As political and economic pressures have resulted in ever larger areas of steppe being turned from grazing land to agriculture, so more and more nomadic tribes have been drawn to adopt an urban way of life. In this new environment, people's allegiance has turned from the tribe to Islam or the Khan, or latterly, to the State. In such a setting many of the traditional textiles become redundant. There is no use in a high-rise apartment for tent-bands. Likewise the traditional motifs are in danger of losing their significance for the people who weave and embroider them, becoming no more than decorative patterns, unrelated to belief. Just as a region closed to travellers since the fifteenth century is opening its gates more widely to the world, the traditional ways of life are rapidly disappearing, and the collection and recording of information about the use of textiles in the live traditions has taken on new urgency.

2 The Materials and Dyes

Sheepskin coats or waistcoats worn with the fleece inside and embroidery or appliqué decoration to the outside were noted by Marco Polo on his Central Asian travels, and are still worn in rural areas today. From the earliest wearing of fur or fleece to the technique of felting was but a short step. The spinning of fibres, fleece and hair to make textiles is believed to have been widespread in the region by the fifth millennium BC.

An unusual textile material observed by Marco Polo on his journey through Eastern Turkestan was asbestos, *salamanda*, mined in the mountains of the Ghinghintalas province. He records that 'when the substance found in this vein has been dug out of the mountain, the particles cohere and form fibres like wool. Then this wool-like fibre is carefully spun and made into cloths [which] when thrown on to the fire turn as white as snow.'

Although in the fourteenth century the energetic ruler Timur encouraged the cultivation of cotton, flax and hemp, of these fibre-giving plants only cotton is suited to the Central Asian climate. There is some local production of linen from flax cultivation and of hemp from the indigenous *Cannabis sativa* of the family *Urticaceae*, as well as of ramie from a plant of the same family, genus *Giradivia*, which grows in the hill country of Eastern Turkestan.

Hair from the Bactrian two-humped camel of Central Asia is valued for its softness, durability and insulation properties. It is collected as the animal moults, and also shorn from the neck and throat. The woven cloth is expensive and a great luxury. The under-layer of goat's hair is strong and soft, and usually makes the warp-yarn for bags, or is carded in with sheep's wool. The long coarse outer coat is used for tough warp-threads or hard-wearing selvedges. Hair from horses' manes and tails makes decorative tassels for the textiles of horse-loving tribes such as the Turkmen, Uzbeks and Kazakhs.

The three main materials used for the construction of textiles, however, are wool, silk and cotton.

(Top) Design from a *suzani* border.

Wool

The earliest sheep indigenous to the steppelands were of the small Dumba stock fat-tailed variety, with a short, downy fleece particularly suitable for felting. Over the millennia selective breeding, mainly for the mutton and sheep-milk produce which is the staple food of the steppe-dwellers, and the intermingling of lowland and mountain breeds resulting from the increased area of migration, have combined to produce the sheep found today. Sheep are bred in vast numbers by Turkmen herders on the steppelands and by Kirghiz nomads in the mountains. The most commonly used wool is from the Karaqul sheep, which has a dual fleece. While the under layer remains short and curled, the outer layer grows a long staple.

Although comparatively minute quantities are produced, worthy of mention is the fleece of a small white sheep with chestnut face, prick ears and small horns. This is reared by the Kirghiz nomads of Eastern Turkestan, and the fleeces are brought for processing to Luktchun, an ancient Buddhist settlement on the edge of the Turfan

Kohistani man spinning fleece with a drop spindle.

lowlands, and to Khotan. 'Turfan wool' has the reputation of being the finest in Asia and is costlier even than silk. The unique sheen of the knotted Khotan carpets is due to its quality.

The excellence of many of the renowned Turkmen and other Central Asian tribal weavings is attributable to a large extent to the fact that the process of yarn-production, from shearing the sheep to the finishing of the article, was and still is done entirely by hand, with a knowledge passed on from master to apprentice.

Shearing takes place out on the grazing-grounds in the spring. Depending on the condition of the flock, there may be a second clip in the autumn. The spring shearing provides the better wool that fetches a twenty-five per cent higher price and is bought for the finer weavings. The sorting of the wool is the key to the quality of the finished article. Experienced hands never mix wool from different parts of the fleece, or from the autumn and spring shearing. Where the process is mechanized, all parts of the fleece, good and bad, go through the system together and the quality is more standardized.

Where wool is produced by nomadic herders, the carding (if this is necessary) and spinning are done during the course of the day by all the members of the community,

Dumba fat-tailed sheep at the annual sheep-fair at Chackcharan, northern Afghanistan.

male and female, young and old. The drop spindle is portable, and can be operated while on the move. The thigh spindle is also used by the women. Wool is chiefly produced and worn in the mountain regions, although there is a small demand for wool in the plains-settlements for the weaving of turban-lengths, *chalmas,* and belts, *futas.*

The women of cotton-weavers' families spin a downy yarn from the soft underfleece of sheep, mixed with similar goats' hair sold in the bazaar by the nomad herdsmen. The spinner boils the down with roots of the plant lucerne to remove the lanoline, then it is dried, spun and kept on the spindle for several days to even out the tension and make it easier to weave. Downy yarn is used only for weft thread, cotton being used for the warp.

Silk and sericulture

There are many legends relating to the discovery of reeling silk fibres from the cocoon of the Bombyx moth. Who is there to dispute the truth of the story of the Empress Hsi Ling-Shi, who around the year 2650 BC, while retrieving a cocoon which had fallen from a branch into her teacup, found that it had unwound in a long filament of silk? Different species of the moth produce different grades of silk, the character of which usually depends on the food source. The finest silk, from which developed the lucrative silk industry, is from the moth *Bombyx mori* which feeds on the white mulberry *Morus alba.* These two varieties co-exist uniquely in north-west China. Silk became the main export of China and was of the greatest importance for the revenue of the country – as also for that of Central Aisa, as initially the only outlet for silk was the overland caravan route.

A speech by the Lord Grand Secretary to the Han Council, recorded in 81 BC, emphasizes the importance of silk for the Chinese trade with the nomad tribes to the north: 'for a piece of Chinese plain silk can be exchanged with the Hsiung-nu for articles worth several pieces of gold, and thereby reduce the resources of our enemy. Mules, donkeys and camels cross the frontier in unbroken lines; horses, dapples and bays and prancing mounts, come into our possession. The furs of sables, marmots, foxes and badgers, coloured rugs and decorated carpets fill the Imperial treasury, while jade and auspicious stones, coral and crystals become national treasures.'

66 (Opposite) Grain- or flour-sack, woven with cotton warps and strong goat's-hair-and-wool wefts, in a patterned stripe of natural wool, madder and indigo.

67-71 (Far left) Knotted-pile bands, piece-dyed in strong madder, indigo, and yellow from the *sparak* plant, making an Uzbek 'bearskin' rug, *dschulchir*. (Left, from top) Kirghiz nomad woman using a hanging spindle. Hanks of wool dyed with indigo and madder, and the brilliance of the original Azo direct synthetic dyes, first imported in the 1880s (hanks at right). Cotton being fluffed up by bowing. Silk filaments being reeled from cocoons by a Ferghana woman.

72 (Above) The red tones so beloved of the Turkmen, varied on a knotted-pile prayer rug. Motifs have been picked out with madder and a local cochineal.

73 Felt dyed with indigo and madder, cut into the shapes of the pattern and appliquéd to felt of natural black fleece.

74 (Right) Detail of a Balouch tribeswoman's kelim. Yarn spun from the fleece of the fat-tailed sheep is dyed to subtle tones of madder and indigo to make the intricate weft-face patterned stripe.

75 Silk twist, dyed to bright colours for exquisite couching-stitch embroidery on a silk hanging for a wall-niche in a Tadjik house.

76 (Right) *Abr* silk, detail of a nineteenth-century bed-cover, *adiol*. Indigo, madder, and yellow from the *sparak* plant have been used pure and in combination to pattern the silk warp-threads, bound and dyed several times before being tensioned on the loom.

77-8 Only chemical analysis can determine a dye-type, but the design of a fabric may date it to a period before or after the introduction of synthetic dyes. The traditional *daira gul* (tambourine) motifs, their soft outlines and the predominance of red, all identify the silk of the woman's *chapan* (above) as made during the nineteenth century in Bokhara, using madder, indigo and *sparak*-yellow. The severe graphic design of the silk-and-cotton *kurta* (right) indicates an *abr* fabric made after 1920, using synthetic dyes.

79 (Below) Geometric blocks of colour identify the man's *chapan* as made in Samarkand at the period when dyers were using both natural and synthetic dyes, or even a combination of the two.

So great was the value of the knowledge of sericulture that legend has it China kept the secret for over two thousand years, until the day came when silkworm eggs were smuggled out of the country. We learn of a Chinese princess who was betrothed to the King of far-off Khotan. Apparently he was a king with knowledge and forethought, for the envoy sent to escort his bride was told to advise 'the Royal Princess of the East' that 'her new country possesses no silk or quilting, and has neither mulberry nor silkworm. These will be needed if she is to have clothes made.' The princess supposedly left China with eggs of *Bombyx mori* and seeds of the white mulberry hidden in her headdress. Once established in Khotan in Eastern Turkestan, and doubtless elsewhere beyond China, sericulture spread westwards along the trade routes to become a lucrative home-industry for town and village households throughout Central Asia.

That silk production was never practised on a large scale owed something to the restrictions placed on the wearing of silk. To be dressed in pure silk clothing was a privilege reserved by edict for the highest in society. Local rulers might encourage sericulture, and ancient mulberry trees, said to be descended from those planted by Timur, may be found today in outlying villages, but the market for silk was a tiny élite, and *kanaus* silk – that is, pure silk – is still called *podshokhi*, 'emperor's cloth'. More widely worn was a mixture of silk and cotton. Only when Central Asia came under Russian rule at the end of the nineteenth century might well-to-do townsfolk wear pure silk clothing for festive occassions.

Today silk production makes use of modern technology, in so far as the reeling process is largely industrialized, and mulberry bushes are planted in large areas and cropped in an efficient way. But the silkworm continues to be a temperamental creature and only thrives on constant care and fresh mulberry leaves. The short season and labour-intensive nature of sericulture make it particularly well adapted to home industry. Turkestan is one of the world's main areas of silk production, and most of the cocoon-rearing is carried on in village houses.

At the end of winter, a few weeks before the mulberry trees come into leaf, a representative from a silk-producing village will travel to a trading centre and buy boxes of silkworm eggs. Since widespread silkworm disease (pebrine) all but destroyed the silk industry of Central Asia, the eggs are now either imported annually from Japan or else bred locally in carefully controlled conditions. Two preferred varieties are the Aloizi (named after a Corsican who opened a silkworm breeding station in Khodzhent in 1892), and the Mandalak (named after a silk merchant of Kokhand). The eggs are distributed to the various households, and incubated by the women who tie them in a cloth pouch, tucked between the breasts for warmth. The hatched caterpillars are put on a platter and fed on young mulberry leaves cut into strips, then, as they grow, are transferred to tiers of wicker trays in a specially built rearing-house to be fed on mulberry leaves on the branch. During its four weeks of life the voracious caterpillar sheds its outgrown skin four times. The process of skin-shedding is a delicate one, and the creature is susceptible to noise, vibration, draughts, strong smells and (reputedly) the presence of pregnant women at this time. When it is 8 to 10 cm (3 to 4 in) long the caterpillar starts to spin a continuous filament of silk held together with gum (sericin), in which it cocoons itself. It starts the cocoon from the outside, and its first efforts are imperfect, hence the outer layer of silk is of lower standard than the filament that lies beneath.

Within ten days, the precise length of time depending on heat and humidity, the metamorphosis of the grub to the moth is complete. It is undesirable that the moth should hatch, as this pierces the continuous filament. Damaged cocoons are processed separately to produce less valuable floss silk used as embroidery thread, or else the shorter, broken filaments are spun. In order to preserve the cocoons whole, they are laid out in the hot sun, which dries them and kills the moth. The cocoons are then sorted, baled and transported to the bazaars, from where they are bought by silk merchants and sent on to the reeling centres.

Until the mid-nineteenth century the task of unwinding cocoons was performed by women in the home, using the *charkh* or spinning-wheel to reel the filament on to bobbins. When silk production suddenly increased and silk-reeling became a profitable trade, men took over the occupation, setting up silk-reeling workshops, known as *pillakashkhona*.

The reeling of the cocoon requires a high level of skill, and is done by the head of the workshop with an assistant. Handfuls of cocoons are thrown into a cauldron of boiling water, heated over a fire of rice husks, camel-dung and stripped mulberry branches, then whisked with a curved stick until they start to produce a loose filament. A pail of cold water is poured into the cauldron to harden the cocoons, to make the separation of the thread easier. The inferior, outer layer of filament, the *pilta*, is first removed. It will later be spun to make embroidery thread. When the good inner filament is reached, the reeler picks up the number of filaments required for the particular denier of yarn to be reeled. The thinnest yarn, made from only four cocoons, will be used to weave fine silk shawls, *dorii*. A thicker yarn, made from sixteen to twenty cocoons, is for heavier silk cloth like *adras* and *kanous*. Several cocoons reeled together when the gum is soft will appear to form a single thread. The art of the reeler is to ensure that the number of filaments reeled together remains constant, so as to give an even denier. If a filament breaks, the reeler must notice that the cocoon has ceased bobbing on the surface of the water, and in an instant, add another thread. The thread is wound on to bobbins via pulleys and a wheel rotated by the assistant.

The cocoons that do not produce ends are skimmed off and sent to a different workshop to be spun as damaged cocoons. The dead moths left at the bottom of the cauldron may be sold to fishermen as bait if the workshop is near a river.

The winding of silk from the bobbins on to small spools is usually done by women of the silk-reeler's family, using an adapted spinning wheel. At the same time any remaining small twigs and dirt are cleansed from the thread.

Twisting of filaments makes a smoother and stronger thread. The *charkhtob*, 'he who rotates the wheel', works alone in a workshop, turning the *devcharkh* – *dev* is a giant of fabled strength. The thread is twisted as it is wound from one set of spools to another, and usually about thirty spools are used at a time. Not all silk thread is required to be twisted, and the *charkhtob* works to order from the weavers.

Cotton

Central Asia is within the cotton-growing belt (45°N-30°S), and where the land is irrigated cotton is grown extensively. The cotton plant *Gossypium* of the Asian short-fibre variety is indigenous to the area, where it is known as *guza* in Western Turkestan and *khiwaz* in the Khotan oases. Early in the history of the oasis settlements the river systems, both to the east and west of the T'ien Shan mountain divide, were utilized to the full, and carefully maintained irrigation channels allowed the cultivation of large oasis areas. Cotton and mulberry trees were grown extensively and supplied raw materials for sericulture and the flourishing textile workshops. A disastrous consequence of the nomad invasions of the thirteenth century was the destruction of the irrigation systems, eventually reducing once-flourishing cities such as Merv, formerly centres of cotton production, to ruins in the desert. The woven cotton cloth of the region was renowned, and was exported to Persia and Byzantium. The production of cotton was gradually re-established during the period of the Khanates, but mainly for the home market.

In the late nineteenth century, when the area was coming under Russian domination, the building of the Karakum Canal and railways promoted intensive cotton production in Western Turkestan to meet the insatiable demands of the Russian spinning and weaving mills. Vast areas of land were irrigated, depriving many nomadic pastoralists of their ancient grazing grounds. In 1880, the long-fibre American cotton variety, locally known as *pakhtai americon*, was introduced. As once earlier towns had mushroomed along the old caravan routes, so now settlements such as Charjui grew up beside the railway tracks for the collection and shipment of cotton.

Practically every farmer would grow some cotton as a lucrative cash crop. The sacks of harvested bolls – ripe cotton seeds – were taken straight from the farms to the local bazaar, where a special area was for reserved for cotton-selling. Most of the production was bought by the wholesale trader who supplied local craftspeople.

Sorting, ginning, breaking and spinning the cotton fibres took place in the home, and enough cotton bolls would be purchased for a week's work. In the autumn, a store would be bought in for winter spinning. The work was performed by the women and children of the family, either outside in the courtyard or in winter sitting around the *sandik* – the central sunken hearth with its brazier.

The woman spinner first fed handfuls of the bolls through a cotton gin or *chirik*, a wooden implement with two grooved rollers that separates the cotton from the seedheads and rolls the fibres. The cleaned cotton was then laid out on a cloth and beaten with rods until it became soft, and the fibres separated – the process known as *pakhtasavvahuni*. Next it was pulled out and rolled between two boards to give manageable bundles (*rolags*), from which it was spun. Most women had two spinning wheels or *charkh*, one for spinning the cotton, the other for plying it on to large bobbins. The spun and plyed cotton yarn was steamed to give an even tension, then wound into hanks and sold to the weaving workshops.

Various grades of thread were spun, often to order, ranging from the finest thread for muslins, to a middle grade used for many different types of cloth including the weft thread for combined silk-and-cotton fabrics, known as *adras* and *bekasab*, to the thick hand-spun thread used for coarse cloth, *karbos*.

A separate process makes the 'cotton wool' used for padding. Usually the poorer grade bolls were chosen, and once separated from the seeds the heaped cotton fibres are fluffed up using the string of a special bow, *kamoni pakhtashapi*. The operators of this process, known as *ting-tingchi*, hire themselves out to any household, workshop or quiltmaker who needs cotton padding.

Dye-sources and dyeing

Many Central Asian textiles use only the natural browns and white of the raw materials to form striped and geometric patterns, but understandably brighter colours have always been widespread. Traditionally dye is applied to spun yarns, whether wool, silk, cotton, linen or bast fibres, and only more rarely to woven fabric. Fleece is dyed before felting. Woven cotton cloth is block-printed with dyes. There is a mystique attached to dyeing, and the skilled dyer has always been held in high esteem by the community. Dye-recipes were sometimes kept secret within a family or workshop and passed down over the generations. The most accomplished workers in the craft are undoubtedly the *abrband* and *ranguborchi*, the men who bind and dye the silk warp-threads for the beautiful *abr* or ikat-dyed fabrics.

Colours play a symbolic role, particularly for textiles used in rites of passage and other ceremonies. When Friar Carpini visited the encampment of nomadic tribes assembled for the coronation of Guyuk Khan in 1246, he noted that 'they had already erected a great tent made of white . . . on the first day they were all dressed in white; on the second day [when] Guyuk came to the tent they were dressed in red; on the third day they were all in blue, and on the fourth day in the finest *baldachins* [silk brocade]'. The predominance of red in the Turkic tribes' weavings and embroideries can be attributed partly to the accessibility of indigenous red-yielding substances, but also to the ancient association of the colour with the life-blood, and vital energies.

The most widespread source of red dye is the powdered root of the madder plant, *Rubia tinctoria*, locally known as *ruyan* (Russian, *mariena*), which is common over the steppelands from southern Afghanistan through Transoxiana and Uzbekistan. The quantity of dye obtained will vary according to the age of the plant, and the roots are dug up in the late autumn when the sap-content is at its lowest. By using the different grades of powdered madder root combined with different mordants, it is possible to obtain a range of colours, from scarlet to violet-brown. Madder cultivated and exported from Central Asia became an important source of revenue during the Khanates, especially in the area around Samarkand and Khokand.

Over such a vast region there are considerable botanical variations, and often particular dye-substances or mordants are specific to the textiles of tribes which frequent an area. In the fertile areas, for example, black is obtained from pomegranate peel, boiled together with iron filings, while in more remote areas, pistachio or a plant of the species *Malvaceae*, locally known as *karachup*, provides tannin required to fix black from iron to yarns or cloth. Unfortunately iron dye hastens the rotting of fibres, with the result that many beautiful weavings have developed blank areas. Numerous plants will give a yellow dye, including safflower, but in most cases this is a fugitive colouring. The most enduring yellow dye comes from an indigenous plant which grows abundantly on the steppe, of the species *Senecio*, but like the European ragwort, it is poisonous to cattle. Florettes of the plant, known by the Uzbeks as *sparak*, and as *zahr-i-choub* (yellow wood) by the Persian-speaking population, are collected in the spring and dried and ground. In the moister, forested mountain regions of the Altai lichens are abundant and are used as dyes, yielding reds and yellows.

Alexander Boris, a lieutenant in the service of the East India Company who travelled in the Oxus region in the 1830s, reported that 'red dye was obtained from spherical worms which lived on the roots of bushes growing on the banks of the River . . .'. This creature, *Margarodes polonicus,* may well be the source of the so-called 'Polish cochineal' that dyed the magnificent knotted carpet found in a tomb at Pazyryk (p. 71), now in the Hermitage Museum, St Petersburg. It is considered the work of highly skilled local tribal weavers, and a long tribal tradition of dyeing and weaving is suggested by the production of so sophisticated an artefact in the fourth century BC.

In eastern Central Asia a deep, vibrant red obtained from the safflower was much valued. Its Chinese name, *Tseng hung hua*, or 'Tibetan red', derives from the guild of dyers who held the secret of the method of extracting red-yielding carthamine from the safflower, and who were established in the mountainous area north of Kashmir. The dye and dyed woollen cloth were exported through the mountain passes to Khotan as part of the Tibetan tributes to China.

The plant *Indigofera tinctoria* from which the blue dye indigo is extracted does not thrive in the dry climate of Central Asia, and blocks of the prepared dye-stuff have long been brought to the area by the caravans from India, and also from Kabul, which was famed for its production.

A distinctive feature of the textiles of nomad steppe-dwellers is the use of simple, intense colours, mainly reds and blue-black. While this can be attributed to the closeness of particular dye-sources and the love of striking effects, it also has a religious connotation, with the sense of combined opposites held in balance – day and night, or good and evil. The more sophisticated settled population, on the other hand, was influenced by the aesthetics of foreign cultures, and regarded the use of the primary colours as primitive, preferring a mixed palette.

Dyeing, like weaving and embroidery, has always been an exclusively female craft in the nomadic population. Young girls learn their skills and the tribal motifs and patterns; but dyeing, as the most elaborate of the processes applied to fleece or yarns, is the last skill to be accomplished. Children gain a knowledge of dye-plants early, as collecting is a family task, but the expertise of mordanting, the heat and duration of the dyebath, and the sensitive combining of colours often takes many years of practise to perfect. Much dyeing, especially with madder which does not require boiling, is done in the embers of the cooking fire, or using the sun as a heat source in the desert areas where fuel is scarce.

In the villages and towns, before the industrial revolution of western Central Asia in the 1930s, the craft of dyeing was organized in small workshops with a master craftsman and three or four helpers, usually young relatives. Particularly in western Central Asia, different methods of dyeing were practised by the various ethnic groups. Dye workshops which require a source of heat were run by Tadjiks and Chala Muslims, former Jews converted to Islam, while the cold indigo-dyeing was performed exclusively by Jews. Both groups worked solely to order. The Jews held the monopoly of the wholesale trade. In a town one particular ethnic group will generally dominate a neighbourhood, and the names of the streets and bazaars indicate their craft. In Bokhara the neighbourhood of Sheikh Rangres, 'The Venerable Dyer', recalls a Sufi saint who amazed his followers by dipping three skeins of yarn into clear water and bringing them out as three different colours.

A few traditional dye workshops can still be found. Most of the space is occupied by a row of clay hearths with copper cauldrons, one for each dye, and further cauldrons contain alum solution for use as a mordant. Firewood is piled in one corner, dried dye-material in another, together with solid alum. In the centre is a raised area, *sufa,* on which craftsmen sit to bind yarns for resist-dyeing for ikat weaving.

Hanks are soaked in alum solution for two to three hours, then hung on a stick to be dipped three times in the cauldron of boiling dye. Next they are re-threaded on the stick, and dipped again three times, to ensure uniform distribution. Finally they are submerged to soak for the required time, according to the particular dye. One worker is responsible for keeping the fires burning at the correct level.

An indigo-dye workshop, where heat is not needed, is chiefly occupied by large clay vessels, *khums,* buried in the ground up to the neck. To ten pails of water are added powdered indigo, slaked lime, iron vitriol and dried mulberry fruits. Twelve or fourteen vats are generally made up, and four are used in sequence, each vat containing a different strength of indigo. Those not in use are tightly capped to exclude air. The yarn is dipped in the vat, drawn out and left to oxydize, when the blue colour develops. The more often this is repeated, the deeper the colour.

Families, tribes and dyeshops have their own tried and tested methods of dyeing, some of which have been passed down over generations. A method of fermentation dyeing with indigo, for example, is traditional for the Ersari Turkmen tribe. For this, a handful of wheat sour dough and sheep or ox bone-marrow are pounded together and put in a vat of water with powdered indigo. The yarn is first soaked in water and barleymeal and then immersed in the vat, which is covered and left outside to ferment in the heat of the sun for fifteen days. Should the dye not be deep enough, more bone marrow and sour dough are added, and the yarn is left to steep for a further period.

The end of the great days of the Khanates and the Russian annexation of Central Asia had a dramatic impact on a craft of dyeing which had been practised little changed since medieval times. When imported synthetic dyes became available in the bazaars in the late nineteenth century, ancient dyestuffs and techniques in which the artisans were confident and skilled were abruptly abandoned in favour of bright colours that were not fast to light or washing, but could be obtained with the ease of opening a packet of powder. The type of the imported dye available depended on the political alignment of the particular area. During the nineteenth century the area north of the River Oxus, for instance, had trading connections with Germany, therefore the first synthetic dyes to reach the market were those developed by the German chemical companies. The Turkmen used a synthetic red dye patented in Russia, while Afghanistan and the valley settlements of the Hindu Kush, which were open to British commerce, used dyes pioneered in Britain. As a result it grew hard to identify a tribal group's textiles by colour alone where pastures straddled a political divide.

3   Felts, Weavings and Dress

Felt, as the most basic manufactured textile, was known to the Central Asian population from earliest times. Wool owes its unique ability to felt to the structure of the fibres, the outer layer of which consists of scales which overlap like roof-tiles, the free edges inclined towards the tip. This structure combined with the elasticity of the fibres, especially when they are warm and moistened with a weak alkaline solution, causes them to interlock and, with pressure, to form a sheet of fabric.

Felts made by the Turkic tribes of Central Asia became renowned in the medieval trading world, but testimony to the early perfection of the craft are the hangings, carpets and other felts discovered in the tomb barrows at Noin Ula in Mongolia and Pazyryk in the Altai mountains. In particular one Pazyryk find, now displayed in the Hermitage Museum, St Petersburg, is a superb coloured felt, depicting two rows of horsemen each of whom is making an offering to a seated goddess. This felt was found in a tomb-chamber early this century, preserved in the permafrost of the High Altai where it had lain buried since the fourth century BC. Appliqué felt decoration was used in the making of this extremely large hanging – from the pictorial arrangement of the design it is thought probable that it was intended to hang vertically.

That felt had all manner of uses is apparent from the other items of felt found in the tombs of the people who populated the valleys of the Altai mountains during the seventh to second century BC. There are covers for the corpses and linings for sarcophagi; socks for men and women; men's outer shirts; cushions stuffed with deer's hair; boots, some embroidered; felt-covered rings used as pot-stands; many patterns of cut-out felt applied as decoration on horses' harness, and ornate horse-blankets. A good riding horse was evidently highly valued, and would be protected from the elements by a felt blanket large enough to cover the back and sides from the ears to the tail, often made in a patchwork of white and brown felt. The same archaeological discoveries show that the technique of rolling felt in different qualities was highly developed at the period – thick, even felts were made for carpets and fine, soft felts for stockings.

Felt itself is credited with protective qualities. Natives of the dry steppelands where scorpions and tarantulas abound believe that these pests will not crawl on to felt. This theory was put to the test by one Gustav Krist who travelled in Turkestan and Tajikistan in the 1920s. He slept on a felt blanket when the camp-area was heavily infested, and 'can testify that I was not bitten nor even touched by one'.

Detail of a felt hanging found in the Pazyryk tombs (reconstruction).

Nomad felts

In the present day, felt is made mainly by nomadic pastoralists in rural areas, where it is used for rugs, jackets and *burka* (the cloaks worn by shepherds), hats, bags, floor- and bench-covers, horse-blankets and saddle-cloths. *Numdah* (felt rugs) have been a product of the Khotan area in Eastern Turkestan for over two thousand years, and large consignments are still exported annually to Ladakh and Kashmir.

For fine quality felt of even thickness only the best downy sheep's fleece is used, never the wool from a dead animal nor from the head or back, which is coarse,

(Top) Weft-face patterned stripe woven in a Balouch *soufreh*, 'eating-cloth'.

although for many rugs, tent-covers and other large utilitarian pieces inferior grades of fleece are adequate. Fleece intended for felting is usually washed on the sheep before shearing, generally by herding the animals through a swiftly running river. Traditionally women do most of the felt-making. The shorn fleece is laid out and beaten with sticks to remove any remaining grit or burrs, and to separate the fibres. If coloured fleece is required, it is dyed at this stage. Sometimes the fleece is carded – that is, bunches are pulled through metal prongs so that the fibres lie parallel. Tufts of fleece are then laid out in layers on a reed mat the size of the required felt. Hot soapy water (originally a variety of the soapwort plant was the cleansing agent) is sprinkled over the piled fleece and the mat and fleece are rolled up as one, then the bolt is rolled back and forth on the ground to compress the wool. This is done by a group of women using the pressure of their forearms, or by two people each pulling one end of a rope, or, in the mountain areas, by a yak harnessed to a pole passed through the bolt to roll it along.

Apart from felt's use in large sheets to make covers for floors, tents or benches, it can be cut as cloth and stitched for shaped garments, or moulded into shape during the manufacturing process for hats and capes.

Felt is the most efficient of insulating fabrics against both heat and cold. Although it has low tensile strength, secured over a self-supporting structure it will withstand the fiercest gale and give excellent protection against the elements. The domed felt-covered tents of the Central Asian nomadic horsemen were recorded by Chinese scribes over two thousand years ago. While their design varies slightly from region to region they all have a similar basic structure. Sections of trellis are lashed together to form a cylinder and encircled with long woven tent-girths which are tied to the post-and-lintel doorway, the number of sections depending on the size of tent required.

Turkmen women rolling felt.

Felt camel-flank trapping, *asmalyk*, of the Goklan Turkmen, embroidered and appliquéd on white felt.

Most commonly a family tent will have five sections, as it is reckoned that each trellis corresponds to one person's living-space. A roof-wheel or crown forms the summit of the dome, linked by curved roof struts to notches in the top of the trellis wall. When the structure is particularly large or there is a heavy load of winter covering, the roof-wheel may also be supported by a pair of central posts. The trellises are made of willow or poplar laths hinged with thongs of raw camel-hide at cross-points, allowing them to be folded down into a neat bundle for transportation. The nomad's tent is commonly known as a *yurt*, which in the Turkic languages means 'home territory' or 'camp site'.

There is much tradition connected with the erection of the tent. When the site is reached, for example, the first act is always to put in place three hearth-stones for the fire. Then the roof-wheel and any furniture are positioned roughly, and the trellis walls are put up in a clockwise order – that is, with the rotation of the sun. Next the door-frame and roof are fixed in position. The layout of the tent interior is protected by rules and taboos, and all the members of the household and the various domestic activities have their traditional places. An invisible line divides the tent, running from the place of honour, the *tor*, to the opposite wall with the entry. To the right of this line is the male side, to the left the female side. The hearth in the centre is sacred. There is a hierarchy in the seating around it, and nothing should ever be passed over the fire. The interior is made colourful and comfortable with woven or felt covers, storage bags suspended from the lattices, embroideries and bedding quilts. Shaped felts cover the ground, and over these are laid felt, flat-woven or knotted-pile rugs.

The felt sheets covering the exterior of the structure are 8 to 10 cm (3 to 4 in) thick, and in the winter several felts are piled on top of one another. Trapezoidal felts, wider at the bottom than the top, cover the sides, held snugly against the trellis by the woven tent-girths or ropes. Over the dome are laid two semi-circular roof-felts, the front panel overlapping the back. Long ties of horsehair rope are thrown over the tent roof and secured to the tent girths. The central roof-wheel, not covered by the roof-felts, has a square cover of felt with strengthening edge-ropes and a long rope hanging from each

Stages in the construction of a nomad family's felt-covered tent or *yurt*.

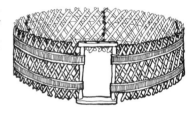

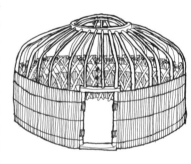

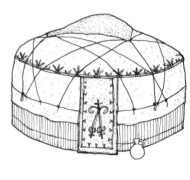

corner. Three secure it, while the fourth rope, at the front, is used to open the flap as an outlet for smoke, or to close it in bad weather or at night, or if a member of the household dies, when it is kept closed as long as the body remains in the tent. A tent covered with newly made felts – usually that of a recently married couple – is white, but the felts gradually darken with smoke and grime. Some tent felts are decorated with appliqué patterns. The door, if not of carved wood, will consist of an ornate trapezoidal felt hung from the lintel.

Embellishment of tents is traditional. A thirteenth-century Chinese account of nomad tents notes that 'the felt around [the] collar on the top they decorate with various pretty designs. Before the entry they also suspend felt ornamented with various

Kirghiz nomads at the entrance to their felt-covered tent.

embroidered designs in colour. For they embroider felt, coloured or otherwise, making vines, trees, birds and beasts.'

Central Asian felts today are decorated with a variety of techniques, some of which allow motifs to take free-flowing forms reminiscent of the ancient Scythian animal designs while others dictate a sharper and more geometrical effect. Patterns may be created by using one of the techniques alone or several in combination.

Widely used by nomadic Turkmen, Kirghiz, Kazakh and Uzbek for making floor- and bench-covers is the procedure known as fulling-in. For this dyed fleece is laid in the required pattern on a background of natural fleece, and the whole thickness is rolled up and felted together.

'Patchwork' felt designs, as the name suggests, are made by cutting out shapes in different coloured felt and stitching the pieces together to form the desired pattern. In western Central Asia distinctive felt patchwork rugs and covers are made by laying felts of contrasting colours, usually red and blue, on top of one another; then the local stonemason uses a sharp knife to cut arabesque patterns through the two, and the resulting shapes are fitted into the contrast-coloured felt, giving positive-negative images. Finally the seams will be overstitched with cord.

Designs are also made when different colours of fleece are layered and felted, then cut through to reveal the colour below. Patterns made by this reverse appliqué technique are usually simple and geometrical, for example a saw-tooth edging, or diamonds or squares.

Appliqué motifs of a variety of materials – felt, cotton, silk, metal or leather – are stitched on to a felt background, especially for the decoration of bags, cradle-felts, hangings, animal-trappings and tent-covers.

Embroidery decorates felt articles while simultaneously strengthening the fabric. Free-flowing motifs are stitched in silk, cotton, metal thread or couched cord in intricate chain stitch, or buttonhole or coral-knot stitches. Often motifs and areas of embroidery are outlined with a contrast-coloured cord. Small discs of felt called *gul-i-peron* (dress flowers) are used for decoration on dress and animal-trappings, and are embroidered with beads, shells and metal thread.

Felts decorated by one or more of these techniques are often further strengthened and ornamented by being quilted on to a cotton backing.

Woven Fabrics

Central Asia, sited between the two prehistoric civilizations of Mesopotamia and the Chinese river valleys and serving as a corridor for the movement of nomadic tribes and travellers, has received a rich and diverse legacy of techniques of yarn-constructed textiles. Over the millennia, nomadic tribal groups and settled populations have evolved and perfected a variety of methods of weaving on a tensioned warp, finger manipulation of yarns, or the use of tablets or hooks or needles to construct a fabric from spun yarn. The earliest evidence of the knowledge of spinning fleece and vegetable fibres has been found in the civilization of Mesopotamia, and the skill will readily have spread through Central Asia with the movement of Neolithic peoples along the Asian land-routes.

The woven textiles of Central Asia may be divided into two broad groups, each characterized by particular types of materials and purposes. Firstly, there are the textiles of the nomadic tribes, with their need for portable furnishings and protection from the harsh elements, and secondly those of urban-dwellers, whose requirement for lightweight clothing in cotton and silk led to very different types of weaving. In the urban or village workshops men were the weavers, for it is not the custom in a Muslim society for women to work in public, although there would be a loom in the majority of houses where women wove to meet the domestic needs of the family. Nomad girls and women will do all the weaving for their group, and the craft has always been highly esteemed, with especially skilled weavers immortalized in legend. Dyeing, spinning and weaving are part of a woman's daily round in nomad and settled communities, although the rhythm of the lives of these two groups varies. For the nomad, the period when the family is settled in the high-valley summer camp allows the looms to be set up on the ground, and the best wool from the spring shearing will be used. For the villagers and urban-dwellers, the summer is a busy time of crop-tending, or cotton-production, or the rearing of silkworms, so that most of the weaving is done in the home during the winter.

Of course in practice there is not always a clear division between the two groups, and many tribal wool rugs will be produced in village communities where semi-nomadic herders live alongside farmers during the winter months. As well as weaving to supply their own domestic needs for floor- and bed-covers, prayer rugs, bands and animal-harness, nomad and village women also weave rugs for sale in the bazaars of the main towns. This fact sometimes makes it difficult to attribute weavings to the tribe or village of origin, since they become known by the name of the bazaar town where they are sold. Thus the early weavings of the Ersari Turkmen became known as 'Beshir' because rugs of this region along the Oxus River were sold in the market of Bokhara, known in the Sart language as 'Bas'chira'.

Until recent times the important role played in the social economy by the dowry ensured that all nomad girls learned the skills and techniques of weaving from their mothers and other women of the family. Betrothal at an early age involved much more than the union of two people. The elders of the bride's and the groom's families were mutually concerned in an arrangement intended to secure the financial and social advantage of both parties. Apart from the joining of water and irrigation rights, or the extension of the grazing area, the exchange of material wealth included most importantly woven textiles, particularly from the bride's side.

Weaving in a mountain village in Kazakhstan. A tripod-frame holds the heddle-rod, simplifying the shed-changing.

Nomad and village weavings

The looms Nomadic pastoralists whose lives are determined by the needs of their animals, moving between steppe and high mountain valley, require portable looms to weave the furnishings for their transient living-spaces. Their loom is a simple horizontal structure of two beams pegged into the ground, between which the warp is tensioned. As the weaving progresses, adjustment is possible by means of various pegs and ropes at the end-beams and along the selvedges. The end-beams are covered with

Balouch nomad woman weaving, seated on a long warp tensioned on rough beams pegged into the ground. The heddle-rod is propped on stones.

Balouch weaver inserting the weft.

clay to prevent the warp-threads slipping. Various tribes have introduced modifications to the basic loom-design – the Turkmen, particularly, favour additional side-beams to form a rigid rectangular frame. So basic a method of holding the warp dictates a narrow width of fabric – up to a metre (about 30 inches) is common for nomad weavings, especially when the unfinished piece is liable to be rolled up and carried to the next grazing-site. Alternate warp threads are passed through heddle-strings suspended from a rod propped on two stones, or hung from a moveable tripod set over the warp. The lifting and lowering of the heddle rod, and the turning of the shed stick, threaded through the warp on the countershed, forms the shed through which the weft is passed. The warp threads are commonly doubled at the outer edges to strengthen the selvedges. If the weaving technique demands individual warp-manipulation, this is simply achieved by picking up the required warps with the fingers. Some tribes use a continuous warp wrapped around both beams, and some use more than one heddle to give a variation on plain (tabby) weave. The weaver sits on the finished part of the weaving, gradually working her way along the warp.

Flat weaves To judge by the textiles unearthed in the Altai tombs, weaving techniques had reached a high degree of sophistication by the first millennium BC. The textiles attributed to local production were exclusively made of fine downy sheep's wool from the type of animal indigenous to the area. Red woollen cloth in both tabby and twill weaves wrapped many funerary articles. Some horse-blankets, *shabrack*, were felt, but many were woven in tapestry, otherwise known as 'kelim' technique, which is thought to have reached Central Asia from Assyria and became widespread throughout the region. In kelim weaving, patterns are formed by the weft threads creating blocks of different colours, none running the full width of the warp. Each colour turns on the borderline with the one adjacent. At the points where the different coloured weft threads meet there are various ways of joining them by interlinkage, or otherwise a slit is left.

The Uzbek weavers who now live a settled existence around Labijar, Maimana, Sar-i-pul and Mazar-i-Sharif in Northern Afghanistan are renowned for their kelim-weave rugs with bold geometric designs.

Traditionally all weaving uses spun wool for both the warp and weft. Some tribes add goat's hair to sheep's wool to give strength to the warp yarn, and some use cotton for the warp. In areas where cotton is grown, particularly around Maimana, all-cotton

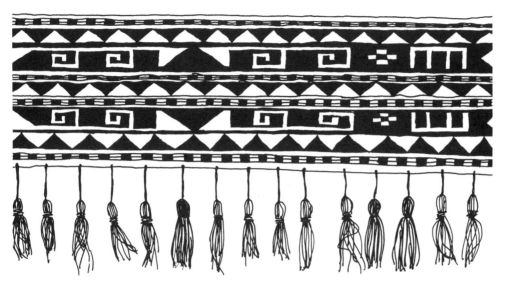

Uzbek tent-band embellished with warp-faced patterns (left and foot of page).

kelim rugs and covers are woven. These are often used in mosques or prosperous households to cover the earth floor and protect more precious wool knotted-pile and flat-woven rugs. In more recent times cotton weavings have been produced by prisoners to earn money to buy food.

Weft-faced and warp-faced patterning are also used throughout Central Asia. Weft-faced patterns are formed by the weft moving from selvedge to selvedge but showing on the surface only when needed to make a pattern of two or more colours, and otherwise floating along the back of the warp. The borders at the ends of the knotted-pile rugs and storage bags woven by the Turkmen tribes are frequently patterned in this way, while the Balouch use the technique for the delicately patterned stripes of their weavings.

For warp-faced patterns the warp is dense, and carefully designed with various colours when being tensioned on the loom. Only the warp threads required for the pattern show on the surface, the others floating on the reverse. This technique is much used by the Uzbek tribeswomen. Only narrow warps can be controlled and tensioned correctly, and the pieces woven have many uses as bands. Uzbek tribeswomen produce *ghudjeri,* covers made from strips of warp-face patterning, ablaze with motifs and detail, stitched together along the selvedges to form large rectangles. Frequently the tent-bands, *baskur* or *iolam,* used to support and strengthen the lattice-tent are woven in this technique. Tent-bands for the interior are often woven on a cotton warp, with a floating silk weft making an intricate pattern, or they may be patterned with knotted-pile weaving interspersed with plain weave.

Weft-wrapping, often called *sumach* or *suzani* (Persian for 'stitch', as it gives the impression of embroidery), is a further flat-weave technique used to pattern rugs and bags. The Kazakh, especially, make large weft-wrapped rugs which are very heavy, as the technique results in many loose ends hanging on the reverse. The Balouch use one or two picks of weft-wrapping to detail a patterned stripe in their weaving.

Knotted pile The knowledge of knotted-pile weaving probably originated in Western Asia, and was further developed by the nomadic tribes who roamed Central Asia, and in particular by the Turkmen who settled in the fertile valleys of the steppeland between the Caspian Sea and the Oxus River. The pile may be left in loops, or else cut

(Below) Spider motif in weft-wrapping, *sumach,* on a plain-weave Kazakh bag.

as a long shaggy pile, or cut and shorn. A fine example of a knotted-pile sheared carpet was found in a fourth-century tomb at Pazyryk. This is designed as a rectangular unit, with a central field of four-rayed stars framed by friezes of griffin, browsing deer and horsemen. The ad hoc solution to the corner-patterns suggests that it was the weaving of very skilled tribeswomen of the Altai region rather than the sophisticated production of an urban workshop. Another piece of pile-weaving from a Pazyryk burial of the sixth century BC is a woollen saddle-cover. From the remaining tatters it is possible to establish that it is of exceptionally fine craftsmanship, and it is also evidence that several types of knotting were in use at this time. Whereas the carpet is constructed of the Ghiordes or symmetrical knot, in which the knot-thread wraps around adjacent warp threads, with three picks of plain weave between each row of knots, the saddle-cover, altogether finer, is constructed with no less than 7,000 Sehna or asymmetrical knots (double that of the carpet) per square decimetre. There are two picks of plain weave between each row of knots, and both the warp and weft are tightly twisted plyed-wool yarn.

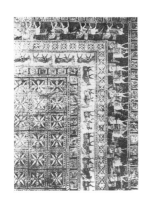

Detail of knotted-pile carpet found in the Pazyryk tombs, fourth century BC.

Other more crudely manufactured knotted-pile textile fragments were found in the Pazyryk tombs, some with an uncut loop, others with a long cut pile akin to the *dschulchir* ('bearskin') rugs still woven today by the Uzbek tribes. The technique of these long knotted-pile rugs differs from that of the Ghiordes knot in that the knot-thread is wrapped round the two adjoining raised warp-threads of an open plain-weave shed. There are usually three picks of weft between each row of knots, so that the same warp-threads carry the knots throughout the woven length, and on the reverse the knots are hidden under the weft. As with most of the nomadic tribal weavings, *dschulchir* rugs are woven on a horizontal loom as a narrow strip (about 30 to 50 cm, 10 to 20 in) which is cut into even lengths to be joined at the selvedge, four or five strips together. The *dschulchir* may be patterned with large-scale geometric motifs, or have a dramatic abstract design created by strips woven in natural wool being piece-dyed in strong primary colours before being stitched together to form a balanced, vertically striped rug.

Tribes who have gradually settled into an urban existence have often retained the individuality of their weavings, although using a wider, more permanent vertical or horizontal loom, frequently sited under a reed-covered shed in the courtyard. This is the case with the Turkmen women, who with the simple equipment of a tensioned warp, a sharp curved knife, a pronged beater and a pair of shears, are supreme mistresses of the craft of knotted-pile weaving. Distinguished by traditional glowing-red dyes in a variety of shades, by their design, tribal emblems (*göl*) and knot-type, are the magnificent knotted-pile carpets of the Salor, Chador, Yomud, Tekke, Saryq and Ersari, sought after by collectors the world over.

The skill of weaving is not only a respected but also a valuable asset among the Central Asian tribes. As well as being a necessity of nomadic existence, the woven rugs are an insurance against hard times. During periods of drought or other hardship the men of the family will clear the home of surplus rugs and weavings and sell them in the bazaar. Merv and Bokhara are two well-known carpet bazaars where for centuries dealers have gathered to obtain bargains. The exception are the precious dowry weavings, such as the flat-woven *kys-gilgam* ('virgin carpet') used to divide the male and female side of the *yurt* or room during the wedding ceremony. These are considered a family's most treasured possession, and their sale would be a last resort.

Fragments of pile carpets dating from the sixth to ninth centuries were found in the sand-buried ruins of Eastern Turkestan, and Khotan is still a centre for knotted-pile carpets today. The town had been prosperous from the earliest times as a centre for jade and gold, mined in the nearby foothills of the Kun Lun range. Around Khotan it is the men who make the carpets. For the weaving they use a variant of the Ghiordes knot in which the knotting thread is wrapped twice round each of two adjoining warp threads, thus making a very firm knot. Nineteenth-century Khotan carpets have a unique feature in rows of knotted-pile appearing on the underside as well as the face. The exceptional sheen of the wool of sheep bred by the Kirghiz in this area, and the rare silk knotted-pile, have made these lustrous carpets an object of desire for wealthy households from China to India and Russia; and despite the difficulty of transporting goods from an oasis town ringed by high mountain ranges, there has been an export trade from Khotan for many centuries.

Covers, hangings, bags and animal-trappings Textiles are woven primarily for utilitarian functions, but also important in the nomad culture is tribal identity, manifest particularly in the decorative appearance of the textiles. Despite the common factors of a simple loom-type, wool yarn and dyes, the weavings of the Turkmen tribes, the Uzbek, Kirghiz, Khazakh, Karakalpak, Balouch and other tent-dwellers of Central Asia, are astonishingly diverse in their structures, colourings and decorative patterns, even when fulfilling similar functions.

Pieces woven to perform the same function often have different names in different areas. *Ensis* and *hatchlu* (Turkic) and *eshik tysh* (Kirghiz), for example, are all names for the felt or woven tent-door hanging. This will usually incorporate protective symbols as motifs among the decorative designs. Especially typical of the Turkmen tribes are the *kapunuk*, the tent-door surrounds, the *germetch* or threshold rug, the *sallanchak* or hanging-cradle, the *kys-gilgam* or tent-divider, and the *ojakbashi*, a U-shaped hearth-surround.

As well as carpets and rugs woven for the floor, bed or bench, there are *namazlyk*, the rugs designed with a central *mihrab*, the traditional arch, and unrolled at the time of prayer, and special funerary rugs, *ayatlyk*. Each makes a clean surface on the desert sand. Similarly, woven squares about a metre (roughly 30 inches) square, known as *soufreh*, are spread out on the ground by nomads and villagers as a surface for the preparation and eating of food. Though in areas where cotton is available these may resemble no more than cotton table-cloths, in wool-weaving areas they are still designed with a central pattern bordered on four sides and woven in intricate flat-weave techniques. The *soufreh* is spread on the ground to receive the bowls of rice and mutton and flat *nan* bread when the family and guests sit cross-legged to partake of the meal. *Soufreh* are also used in the essential daily task of making bread. The grain is ground over the *soufreh-i-ard* (*ard* meaning flour), and the dough is mixed on the cloth. The four corners are drawn up, and the covered ball of dough is left to settle. Often a village family will take their day's supply of prepared dough wrapped in the *soufreh-i-nan pazi* (bread-bake cloth) to the communal bakery, where the *nan* are shaped and baked and then stacked on the cloth with the four corners pulled up to cover them, to be collected in the evening by the family, with the number of *nan* recorded on a tally-stick for future payment to the baker. The nature of their use means that every-day *soufreh* become soiled with dough and grease, and so older traditional examples are rare. But the *soufreh* woven to be laid on the ground for the banquet at a wedding or other ceremonial occasion, which are often large, are preserved as superb examples of the intricacies of nomad weaving.

Another type of woven square is the *soufreh-i-ru-korssi* ('cloth to cover fire'), shortened to *rukorssi*. These covers are specific to the settled life-style, and are used during the cold winter months when house-dwellers keep warm round the *sandik*. This is a bowl or brazier containing slow-burning charcoal which is placed in a pit in the earthen floor of the communal room of the house and covered with a wooden or metal frame draped with felt or quilts. The family, most frequently the women members, sit round with their feet in the pit and legs tucked under the quilt. The *rukorssi* is placed over the felt or quilt as a decorative centre-piece; or it makes a table-cloth, or cloth to hold fleece for spinning, or threads for embroidery – activities which take place around the *sandik*. Nomads, with fires built of fast-burning camel dung, scrub grass and thistles rather than charcoal, have no use for the *sandik* and its decorative cover.

80 Felt floor-cover, *numdah*, with free-flowing Kirghiz pattern. It is made by the 'fulling-in' method, in which dyed fleece is laid on top of a layer of natural fleece, according to the desired pattern, and the two layers are rolled and felted together.

81 (Left) Turkmen felt rug with pattern of 'positive-negative' images. The shapes for the pattern are cut out from two overlaid sheets of felt of contrasting colours, then the coloured pieces are exchanged and the edges oversown.

82 Lakai felt floor-cover. Appliqué and fulled-in motifs on a backing of dark felt have been further enriched with silk couching stitch.

83-4 Turkmen felt bags, *boche*. Squares of cloth with the four corners folded to the centre are widely used to carry all manner of objects, from flat nan bread-loaves to the Koran. Seams are strengthened with embroidery over braid.

85 (Below) Yomud Turkmen horse-blanket, intricately embroidered in silk lacing stitch (*kesdi*), chain and cross stitch – evidence of the high regard for the horse among the steppe tribes.

86-8 Ceremonial felts. (Above left and above) Fine *okbash*, the pointed bags used in pairs to cover the ends of the folded tent-roof struts, embroidered and appliquéd with cotton fabric for the dowry. (Top) Camel's felt head-harness, embellished with wrapped cords and tassels.

89 (Left) Small triangular felt trapping, appliquéd with cotton, to be worn by an animal or hung over the tent-door.

90 Turkmen woven horse-cover, of dyed wool on cotton warps, magnificently patterned with weft-wrapping, *sumach*. The backing-layer is thick felt.

91 (Right) Rug woven in slit-tapestry or kelim technique, a method producing clearly defined geometric shapes. Each region has distinctive patterns and colours. This example is from the Maimana area in northern Afghanistan.

92 (Far left) The nomad's simple loom, two beams pegged to the ground, restricts the number of warp threads that can be manipulated to weave warp-face patterns. To surmount the limitation larger covers are made up of long bands, cut to length and joined at the selvedges, like this Uzbek *ghudjeri*, a general-purpose cover.

93 (Left) Balouch rug, in the tones of madder and indigo so beloved of the tribe. The intricate weft-face patterned stripes are varied with areas of knotted-pile.

94 (Right) Village prayer rug from north-east Afghanistan, with motifs of knotted pile woven in a tabby-weave background. The design is unusual for an Islamic artefact in representing the human form.

95-6 Traditional storage-bags, illustrating the tribeswomen's extraordinary weaving skills. (Top) Wide Uzbeck bag, *juval*, with a raised pattern of weft-wrapping in coloured silk on plain-woven cream wool. (Left) Turkmen bag for storing clothes, with knotted-pile face displaying the tribal *göl*.

97 (Above) Salt-bag, *namakdan*, with a long neck to fold over and preserve the precious contents from spillage.

98 (Top) Yomud Turkmen *jallar*, storage-bag, skilfully patterned with *sumach* weft-wrapping. The top fastens with a band of loops, each loop threaded through the next to make a chain.

99 (Left) Small Kirghiz bag, ornamented with star motifs in *sumach* weft-wrapping.

100 (Below) Uzbek Tartari pannier-bags, *khurjin*, worked in interlock tapestry-weave.

101-2 Uzbek 'bearskin' rugs, *dschulchir*, woven with the very long pile that is believed to represent the earliest form of the knotted-pile technique. Designs vary according to the subtribe, from bands dyed in strong colours and joined at the sides to give balanced stripes (left), to considered geometric patterns (above).

103-4 (Opposite) The intricacy of patterns and weaving techniques belies the utilitarian use of *soufreh*, woven squares which are laid on the ground to make a clean surface for the preparation or eating of food. (Above) Uzbek *soufreh*, made up of narrow warp-face woven bands. (Right) Balouch *soufreh* incorporating both weft-face patterned stripes and knotted pile, on the same warp.

105-6 The skills of knotting and braiding embellish and strengthen every kind of object and trapping. Long cords and tassels swing pendulum-like with each movement of the animals or their loads. (Left) Horse's rump-harness, sewn with buttons and shells. (Below) A panel of wrapped cords and tassels to decorate a tent-band.

107 (Opposite) Tent-bands, *baskur* or *iolam*, the girths that encircle the trellis-wall of the nomad's tent. Four Uzbek bands are exquisitely woven in silk and cotton. A Turkmen band (far right) is handsomely made with warp-face patterned wool.

108 (Opposite below) Holder for a nomad-woman's cooking-spoons. The mesh is formed of four-strand flat braids, moving obliquely and interlacing at crossing-points, with a fringe of square-knot cords ending in a row of tassels.

109 (Above left) Hazara knitted designs of stylized tulips, stars and running water. Both men and women knit, especially in the cold climate of the high mountain villages.

110 (Above) Heel-less socks worn inside the boots of the *chopendoz*, Turkmen riders of *boz-kashi*, the game of 'catch goat'.

111 (Left) Traditional patterns decorating socks and slippers from Afghanistan. They are now knitted chiefly for export, using wool unravelled from old garments received as foreign aid.

Lacking vegetable fibres to make baskets and wood for furniture, nomads turn to woven bags (known generally as *kep* throughout Central Asia) to store and transport their possessions. The wealth and status of a family is judged by the number and quality of the bags that hang from the lattice of the tent to store clothing, bedding, domestic items and hunting equipment, or are slung from sides of camels, horses and donkeys when the tribe moves camp. The *göl* and decorative patterns woven on the bag-face are the badges of tribal identity.

Various shapes of bag and types of fastening have developed for specific uses. The precious commodity salt is carried in the *namakdan*, a distinctive small square bag with a long narrow neck which folds over to prevent spillage. Fine bags are made to hold the Koran, and small bags adorned with tassels to carry medicinal earth. The names *shabadan* (Kazakh), *karshin* (Karakalpak), *chavadan* (Kirghiz), *juval* (Hazara), *madrach*, *chuval* and *jallar* (Turkmen) all refer to the bag which is used for storing and carrying the family's goods. Usually large, the bags fasten with cord loops, threaded through slits in the opposite top edge, and chained, that is, secured by threading each loop on the one following. Frequently decorative fringes and tassels hang at the sides and along the bottom edge, and identical pairs are woven to hang on each side of a pack-animal.

Pannier-bags, known as *khurjin* – the spelling and pronunciation vary in the different dialects – are made by every tribe. They are woven as one long piece with patterned end-squares to be folded to the centre and sewn up, so that the traditional decorative motifs show on the outside of the pannier. The under-section is usually a plain weave or simple stripe. Panniers are made in many sizes to be slung over pack animals or carried on people's shoulders or, today, on the bar of a bicycle. They may hold a shepherd's midday meal, a newly-born lamb, or animal-feed, household goods, or merchandise for the bazaar. The tradition of using woven bags to transport goods persists to the present day. It is common at a bus stop or lorry *serai* to see the corded loops being carefully chained along the bag-opening, and a metal padlock fastened through the last loop.

Their animals are the nomads' greatest asset, and they are treated accordingly. Many items of harness and animal-trappings will be woven for a girl's dowry. They may include superb *asmalyk*, the decorative flank-covers for the camel; *deslik*, a collar for the lead-camel of the wedding caravan, later hung over the tent-door with the back displayed to show the bride's weaving skill; *okbash*, long bags gathered to a point, from which hang elaborate wrapped and tasselled cords, woven in pairs and used to cover the ends of the tent-roof struts when they are carried on either side of the camel; camel knee-covers; the wedding-litter canopy; the groom's saddle-cover; and above all the amazing camel-halter constructed of crown knots of wool yarn made over a core, cleverly forming a chevron pattern, and obliquely plaited flat-braids. Decorated with pom-poms, tassels, buttons, cowrie shells and blue beads, these trappings contribute much to the pomp and ceremony of the wedding procession.

Decorative finishings

The skilled craft of knotting and braiding was highly developed and used in all manner of decorative forms early in Chinese history, and the knowledge travelled westwards along the trade routes through Central Asia. Braided hair and horsetails were found in the Pazyryk burials, together with dress-girdles of four-sided crown sinnets knotted in plyed wool.

The warp ends of woven rugs, covers and bags are finished in a variety of ways, to strengthen and decorate the articles. On bags and trappings which sway with the movement of the pack animals, woollen warp ends are generally braided in flat-braids or sinnets, or wrapped and decorated with tassels, cowrie shells, blue beads and metal discs. Braided wool is also used for ropes and belts, and to make a fabric, when it is usually shaped into a bag with a construction of a row of eight-element square braids which begin over a stretched cord. As the braids are worked downwards they move obliquely and interlace with the neighbouring braid, forming a dense net. The bag will be used to hold long wooden spoons or other cooking utensils.

Tassels may be very elaborate, made of skeins of wool, silk or horsehair wrapped over a core of cloth to give a full 'head'. Some tribes, the Balouch in particular, decorate them with skilful knotting akin to macramé. Coloured threads are fixed to the central cord at the head of the tassel, and are knotted with the appropriate colour with a half-hitch over a binding cord tensioned from the big toe of the craftsman or woman, while being slowly turned round the tassel-head. The most elaborate pattern, a lozenge-shape, is known as 'wild ass eye', and is reserved for the decoration of special weavings.

Knitting and crochet

Knitting is practised throughout Central Asia. Both men and women in mountain villages are keen knitters of socks, pullovers and hats worn for protection during the harsh winters. The Hazara, especially, decorate their knitting with the use of two colours in any one row, with the colour necessary for the pattern brought forward for the stitch while the second colour floats behind. Four needles are used, and the garments are knitted in a circular fashion. The ancient horn-patterns and stylized floral motifs make these garments very decorative. In recent times a home industry has developed with the knitting of slipper-socks stitched to a thin leather sole for export to Europe and the USA. In a curious cycle, these are knitted from wool which is unravelled from garments sent as aid from the richer nations to underdeveloped countries.

A hook is used, crochet-style, to form a very dense fabric of an ingenious single-element interlooped structure, to make another type of sock. A firm band of looped yarn holds the heel-less tube round the calf of the wearer and the sock tapers to a point at the foot. Such socks are worn inside high leather riding-boots, and are often referred to as *boz-kashi* socks, in reference to the very elaborate examples made for the riders (*chopendoz*) of *boz-kashi*, 'catch-goat', the game so popular with the Turkmen horsemen.

Weaving of the urban-dwellers

Although weavers of the neighbouring regions of China, India and Persia used the advanced techniques of the drawloom to make brocades, these looms were never widely established in Central Asia. From early times ornamented silk brocades and damasks were much beloved of the Uzbek aristocracy, but most were imported rather than woven locally. The four- and eight-shaft pit loom which was so widely used in India became the standard domestic and small workshop loom throughout the cities, towns and larger villages of Central Asia. The frame of the loom is constructed over a pit in the floor where pedals to change the heddles are operated by the weaver's feet, leaving both hands free to pass the weft-shuttles and greatly speeding the weaving-process.

Weaving in the towns and lowland villages was mainly of cotton cloth, worn by people of every ethnic origin and status throughout the warmer areas of Central Asia. Silk cloth was also produced in limited quantity, and especially the fine silk, *doroi*, used to make the semi-transparent shawl or scarf worn by Muslim women in all parts of Central Asia. As the oasis towns gained in prosperity, so the production of luxury cloths, fine cottons, ikat silks and embroideries for the attire and furnishings of the courts, developed into a significant industry.

After centuries of repeated waves of nomad invasion, the establishment of the Khanates and the rule of the Uzbek emirs in the late seventeenth century opened a

Pit loom, worked with treadles in order to leave the weaver's hand free. Warp threads are tensioned with bags of sand.

period of inward-looking cultural development. With the opening up of sea-trade routes Central Asia was no longer to the same extent a crossroads of international trade and influence. Tyrannical rulers, concerned to remain all-powerful, encouraged xenophobia and religious fanaticism, thus creating a culturally isolated society. Textile workshops were patronized to provide symbols of power and wealth in the form of furnishings and dress for the courts. Set up in the vicinity of the palaces of cities such as Bokhara, Khokand and Khiva, they created sumptuous fabrics and embroideries, the type of cloth and the technique of weaving a measure of the wearer's status. Crafts guilds were revived to regulate production and trade, and to protect the interests of the craftsworkers.

Bokharan Jewish merchants wearing the traditional striped-cotton *chapan*.

Cotton-weaving

The weaving of cotton cloth was the most common domestic handicraft of the oasis towns and villages until the nineteenth century. Almost every household possessed a loom for the manufacture of cotton cloth for the making of garments, turbans and girdles, as well as coarse calico for the family's use and for sale in the bazaar. Records of oasis trade indicate the high quality of the cotton cloth exported to Iraq, Persia and India and distributed to the rural areas of Central Asia, and show that, until the early nineteenth century, woven cotton was an important element in the trade between Central Asia and Russia.

Woven cotton fabrics displayed regional variations in the designs and colours. Patterns were largely restricted to stripes and checks, but with a sophisticated application of stripe-width and colour-balance. A few centres, such as Nurata, produced cloth with a combination of plain stripes and ikat-dyed stripes – stripes produced by tie-dying the warp-threads before weaving. *Yalangdavron*, a brightly coloured ikat-dyed striped cotton produced in Khodzhent, was the most popular fabric with the Kirghiz people of the steppe, who used it for headscarves and girdles.

The finish of the cloth was important. For some cloth used for dress material finish by glossing was part of the fabric production, and weavers from the surrounding area would bring woven lengths to the *kudunggari* or glossing workshop. The process of glossing involved the cloth being soaked in the foam of white of egg, beaten with wooden hammers, and pressed between flat stones. This gave a stiffly starched fabric with a distinctive moiré effect.

Many different types of woven cotton were developed. The most widely distributed coarse cotton cloth, *karbos*, was made of hand-spun yarn that had been boiled and starched before being threaded on the loom. The weft was thicker than the warp, and was continually moistened to facilitate the weaving process. *Kalmi*, another coarse-woven cotton fabric, was patterned with finely spaced stripes, blue and white stripes being popular with the Tadjiks and Uzbeks, red and black with the Kirghiz. A denser cloth, *koki*, meaning 'dry', was woven with thick hand-spun yarn in the dry state. In the early twentieth century *koki* was still being produced by a large group of weavers in Khodzhent. It was used for *suzani* embroideries, and was much in demand among the Kazakh and Kirghiz.

Gradually, as machine-spun yarn from the Russian spinning factories became widely available, it was combined with hand-spun yarn to produce some interesting cloths. One, *salori bulur*, was woven in the natural colour, white, and was given a texture by combining thick and thin threads in the warp. It became popular around Khodzhent for brides' garments. A light muslin, *patis*, made from machine-spun yarn in the warp and weft, was produced in Samarkand. Much of this was sent on to another workshop to be bleached in a solution of potash and lime. Known as *khosa*, the fine white cloth resulting was used for turbans (*chalma*) and shrouds. Cloth of similar weight woven with a contrasting blue weft was also popular as a turban fabric. *Alocha*, a fine cotton cloth in a variety of coloured stripes and frequently worked with a coloured weft, was used for men's coats (*kalat* and *chapans*) and for linings. It is manufactured in factories and is popular over a wide area today.

From the late nineteenth century the Central Asian market became flooded with cheaper cotton materials from the Russian factories, so producing near-total unemployment among the local weavers. The resourceful urban workshops increased the production of a silk-and-cotton fabric which was in demand at the time as a novelty for export to Russia. *Bekasab* is a dense cloth with silk warp-threads and a thicker cotton weft; usually woven in twill, which gives the characteristic diagonal line in the weave, it became popular for men's *khalat* and *chapans,* and women's and children's clothing throughout Central Asia. As with the handwoven all-cotton fabrics, silk-and-cotton weaves are varied and have regional characteristics. The combination of wide and narrow stripes in the cool green and violet characteristic of Ferghana is still popular throughout Uzbekistan. *Bekasab* manufactured in Samarkand includes cotton in the warp, giving a dull stripe which sets off the sheen of the silk stripe. One fabric, called *mushku-zafar* ('musk and saffron'), has very dark, blue-black stripes of cotton and yellow stripes of silk warp which shine like metallic thread. This fabric is often used for the bridegroom's wedding-robe.

Contrasting colours and yarns in warp and weft are used to give a fabric a 'shot' effect, a popular combination being that of extremely narrow stripes of white silk and dark-blue cotton, woven with a dark-blue weft, named *paripasha*, – 'fly's wing'.

Pomegranate-flower and ram's horn design, ikat-dyed and woven in silk.

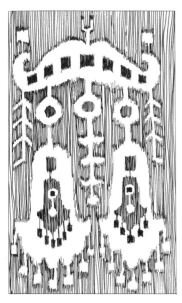

Ikat silk-weaves

Early references to Central Asian commerce document the silk trade and the production of silk, although it is not until the eighteenth century that evidence appears of ikat-dyed silk cloth. While silk-production centred on Khotan in Eastern Turkestan had been an important industry since the sixth century, production of silk elsewhere in western Central Asia was in slow decline through several centuries of civil strife and turbulence until the period of the Timurid Empire in the mid-fourteenth century, when it gradually revived. A vital silk industry was re-established by Shah Murad in the Zarafashan valley, north of Bokhara, in the 1770s. From this date forward the provision of sumptuous cloths for the ruling families of the oasis towns gave renumerative employment to textile craftsworkers. Of all the extravagant adornments commissioned for the Emirs, it was the ikat-dyed silks, and above all the ikat-dyed silk velvets, that became renowned worldwide. These silks – known as *abr* (Persian, 'cloudlike') – are the most visually dramatic woven textiles of Central Asia. Produced chiefly in Uzbekistan, and characterized by shimmering, soft-edged designs in vibrant colours, they owe their beauty to the technique of binding and dyeing the patterns on to the warp threads before they are set on the loom. Like clouds, the motifs appear to float unbounded, their edges softly blending into the adjacent colours.

Although the introduction of Central Asian *abr* silk fabrics is relatively recent, and this unique cloth was made for Muslim patrons, nonetheless the *nishonzan* or ikatdesigners chose their motifs from an artistic tradition several thousand years old. Pomegranates, tulips, rams' horns, scorpions, and other motifs according to the region of production, are stylized but still recognizable. Frequently designs are of a single motif on different scales. Workshops developed individual styles, and cloth may be recognized as originating in a particular area. *Lola gul* (tulip), *kutch karagul* (ram's horn), *daira gul* (tambourine), and *shona gul* (comb-flower), are typical designs from Bokhara, with reds and yellows predominating. The designs of Ferghana and Khojent *abr* are smaller and less dramatic, and more subdued in colour. One, named *kychik* (tickling), is a cheerful zigzag pattern. The *abr* of Samarkand are simpler, relying on blocks of colour for effect.

During the early post-revolutionary years *abr* designs broke away from the traditional representational forms and became more abstract, almost like stains. Some workshops were reluctant to break with tradition, however, and formed more abstract patterns by immense enlargement of repeat, which might often reach a length of 2.5 metres (over 8 foot).

Ikat-dyed silks, until the early twentieth century worn only by the aristocracy or well-to-do merchant families.

The technique of applying *abr* patterns is complicated and was mastered by a limited number of craftsmen, known as *abrband*. Each part of the process was performed in specialized workshops. A length of cloth would usually be commissioned by a merchant or wealthy individual, who would pay the craftsmen at each stage.

First the silk threads of the warp-length of 240 metres were wound with crosses in the usual way, and then divided into hanks or *livit*, which might be of no more than ten threads each. To keep the *livit* in order, the warp was carefully wound between two rods set the length of the design-repeat apart. The winding usually formed about eighty layers. The characteristic white mark which shows at intervals across *abr* fabric is caused by the fold where the rod presses against the warp, causing it to resist the dye.

The *livit* is carried to the *nishonzan* ('he who puts the marks') who applies dots of charcoal ink to mark each of the bundles of warp where it should be dyed. The parts of the warp to be reserved from that particular dye-bath are then bound tightly with thread. The bundles of warp are next taken to the *ranguborchi*, the hot-dyers, and immersed in the first colour – usually the palest yellow. The process is repeated, working from the lightest to the darkest shades. Between each dyeing the warp-bundles are washed, dried in the sun and re-bound to preserve the already coloured portions. Indigo blue, dyed in a cold vat in a special workshop, was the last colour to be applied. Seven colours might commonly be achieved with natural dyes, by dyeing in pure colour and then overdyeing, but *abr* silks with patterns of nine colours were the most valued.

After the elaborate preparation of the warp, the weaving process is comparatively simple. A two- or four-heddle loom is threaded, and it is the job of the *ishtibar* to supervise the workshop and adjust the patterns of the warp-threads while weaving takes place. In many workshops *abr* silk was woven in tabby (plain) weave with a white cotton weft, making a fabric widely known as *adras*. If the weft is hidden in a dense warp-faced weave, the ikat resist-dyed pattern stands out clearly. If, on the other hand, the warp is not so closely threaded, the thicker cotton weft shows as a horizontal rib. *Adras* fabrics might be finished by glossing. Popular in the Bokhara area were *abr* silks woven with a pink silk weft which gave a rosy hue to the entire fabric. The finished cloth was narrow, measuring 26 to 30 cms (10 to 12 in) and this determined the cut of clothes made from it.

Some specialist workshops produced twill-weave *abr* fabrics, others a satin-weave known as *atlas.* One of the last of the Emirs of Margellan was particularly fond of a very dense all-silk satin-weave *abr* fabric which thus became known as *khan atlas.* It was woven on a complex threading of eight heddles, so that the ikat-dyed warp gave a clear pattern in the smooth satin-weave surface.

(Right) A rare example of a silk-velvet tablet-woven belt.

Early in the nineteenth century, at the height of production of luxurious fabrics, there appeared silk-velvet ikat, *baghmal*, the most costly and exclusive weave of all. For the manufacture a complex threading of a double warp was necessary. A foundation-warp of plain orange or pink silk threads was threaded alternately with an ikat-dyed warp several times the length of the plain warp and set on a separate beam. As the weaving with a cotton weft progressed, the ikat-dyed warp was raised separately over grooved wires inserted on alternate picks. After a section was woven, a sharp blade was run down the grooves, leaving the velvet pile with its clear ikat pattern held by the alternate pick of cotton weft.

Abr silk was used for clothing, for wallhangings, *pardah*, which were made of joined panels and often combined fabrics with different designs, for curtains for doorways, and for tent-walls at festive outdoor gatherings. Bed-covers, *adiol*, made of padded quilted cotton, were often covered with *abr* fabric. Such covers were used throughout Central Asia and were a popular item of export to Russia during the nineteenth century.

During the Khanates very fine twill-woven *adiol* were made as decorative wedding-night bed-covers. The warps were generally tied to give a large rosette of concentric circles, and often dyed in pale colours. A white silk weft gave a silvery sheen to the weave, which was known as *shokhi-bargikaram* – 'the silk of cabbage leaves'.

Until the nineteenth century the production of silk cloth had effectively been limited by the restrictions applied to its wearing. To be clothed in pure silk was considered the exclusive privilege of the aristocracy. Not until after the annexation of Central Asia by Russia and the subsequent overthrow of the Uzbek rulers, did silk fabric come into more general use.

Sugra Kasimova, a grand old lady of present-day Bokhara, describes how in her youth *abr* silk coats (*khalat*) were worn by the well-to-do townsfolk for weddings and festivals, and as formal visiting dress. Her father was one of the Emir's generals, and she can remember twelve men weaving in the courtyard of their house. By 1929, all the craft workshops catering to the aristocracy had been closed down, and many of the artisans had fled to Afghanistan or Iran. To supply the expanding market throughout Russia, cloth production generally was organized on factory lines, with no place for the labour-intensive techniques of *abr* silk. The popular demand for ikat-patterned fabric was met largely by machine-printed 'faux-ikat', coloured with synthetic dyes.

During the 1960s there was a revival of warp-patterned fabric produced in factory conditions with simplified, severely geometric motifs in two or three bright synthetic dye-colours, often painted on to the warp with a brush. With trade-names like 'Kremlin' and 'Sputnik', the fabric became widely available. Nowadays factory production of *abr* silk on semi-mechanized looms is well established in Khojent and Margellan in Ferghana, and the modern version of the cloth of Khans is popular as a dress fabric with the newly emancipated women of Central Asia.

Dress

Central Asian styles of dress are as various as the ethnic origins of the people. Tribal groups living in remote valleys or travelling the desert wear distinctive costumes, often richly decorated with embroidery and amulets, and gathered or stitched with many gussets to give fullness and freedom of movement.

The dress of villagers and urban-dwellers, the Turkmen, Uzbek, Tadjik, Sarts and Jews, is more uniform in cut, but no less varied in embellishment, colour and weave of cloth, according to the wearer's ethnic group, religion and status.

Full drawstring trousers tapering to the ankle originated in Central Asia as a practical garment to wear on horseback, and are worn by both sexes. Men wear a loose cotton shirt and frequently a waistcoat, which may be embroidered. A girdle, *futa*, of a length of cotton fabric is worn wrapped round the waist, and serves as a 'pocket' to hold a purse or tin of *neswar* (snuff), or may be spread on the ground as a prayer-mat. Several different types of overcoat are in common use, to suit the climate and occasion. There is the *chapan*, a loose coat of padded and quilted cotton; the *postin*, a fur or sheepskin coat, either embroidered on the outside, or, for the well-to-do, made of brocade or silk and lined with fine lambskin. The *khalat* is a loose, thin, long-sleeved overcoat of cotton or perhaps ikat-dyed silk. Several are often worn at a time, thrown cloak-like over the shoulders.

Prosperous Islamic rulers would give *sar-o-par* (head-to-foot) sets of clothing, of a value according to status, to each member of the court at the New Year. Silk *khalat* were also presented as robes of honour to guests or given as a reward for service to the Emir. Nineteenth-century travellers recorded receiving many robes during the course of their visit, and often sold them to merchants who came to the court.

The *khalat* was bordered with patterned-silk edging-tape, *zeh*, stitched on to the coat material. This might be embroidered or tablet-woven. In the towns and villages of Uzbekistan, intricately patterned narrow widths woven with tablets were also worn as belts and used as bands. The height of technical achievement were the exquisite patterned tablet-woven bands of velvet. A third type of edging for the *khalat* is made by an ingenious method of loop-manipulation. Warp threads placed around the border of the coat are looped on the fingers of one or more people (the number depending on the complexity of the pattern), who then use the movements of their fingers to change the shed. Another helper inserts the weft, threaded on a needle and stitched through the coat and lining on the return pick.

Embroidery embellishes the leather boots made and sold by cobblers in every bazaar, and worn by wealthy Uzbek women.

Unlike the countrywomen, the women of the towns adhere to the Muslim rule of wearing a veil when in public. This may be anything from a fine silk shawl, *rumol*, to a thick veil of horsehair worn by the Turkmen women, or a long pleated *chowderi* with a netted eye-hole. The *chowderi* completely covers the woman's garment, the *kurta* (tunic), which in the case of married women has a front opening to facilitate breast-feeding. The colour and decoration of the *kurta* varies from group to group. Turkmen women are particularly fond of red, and hang the bodice with metal discs and jewellery. Under the *kurta* are worn drawstring trousers.

Various styles of coat or jacket are worn over the *kurta*, the most notable being the Turkmen *chyrpy*, worn like a cloak over the shoulders or the head with long embroidered vestigial sleeves hanging down the back. False-sleeved robes have a long tradition in Central Asia, and are common to both male and female costume.

A significant item of identification is the headgear, and nomadic tribes have individual styles. The Turkmen, for instance, wear large shaggy sheepskin hats, the Kazakh fur, and the Kirghiz sleek moulded-felt hats. For ceremonial occasions women's headwear is very elaborate, with embroidery and jewellery. The style varies with the tribes, but cover for vulnerable parts of the body such as the nape of the neck and the long plaits of hair is a common feature. Protective hats, frequently hung with amulets, are made for newborn infants. A common basic structure upon which elaborate additions are stitched is the skull cap. Caps vary in pattern according to the region, tribe or religious group, and much importance is attached to the type of embroidery and decoration. Muslim men wear skull caps indoors to cover a shaven head, and wrapped beneath a long turban when in the street or travelling. The manufacture of turbans is carried on by *futabof* (cotton-turban makers) and *sallabof*, (silk-turban makers). As with the skull cap, the type of turban identifies the ethnic group, class, religion and area of domicile of the wearer. Silk turbans were and are only worn by the aristocracy and are extremely finely woven. A popular design is a very small indigo-and-white check called *chashmi buldul* – 'nightingale's eyes'.

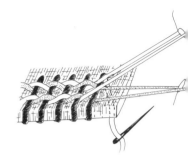

Loop-manipulation to make silk edging-tape, zeh.

112 (Opposite) Detail of an Uzbek *kelim-suzani*, 'embroidered flatweave'. Warp-face patterned bands alternate with boldly embroidered plain-weave to form a sophisticated and skilfully executed design.

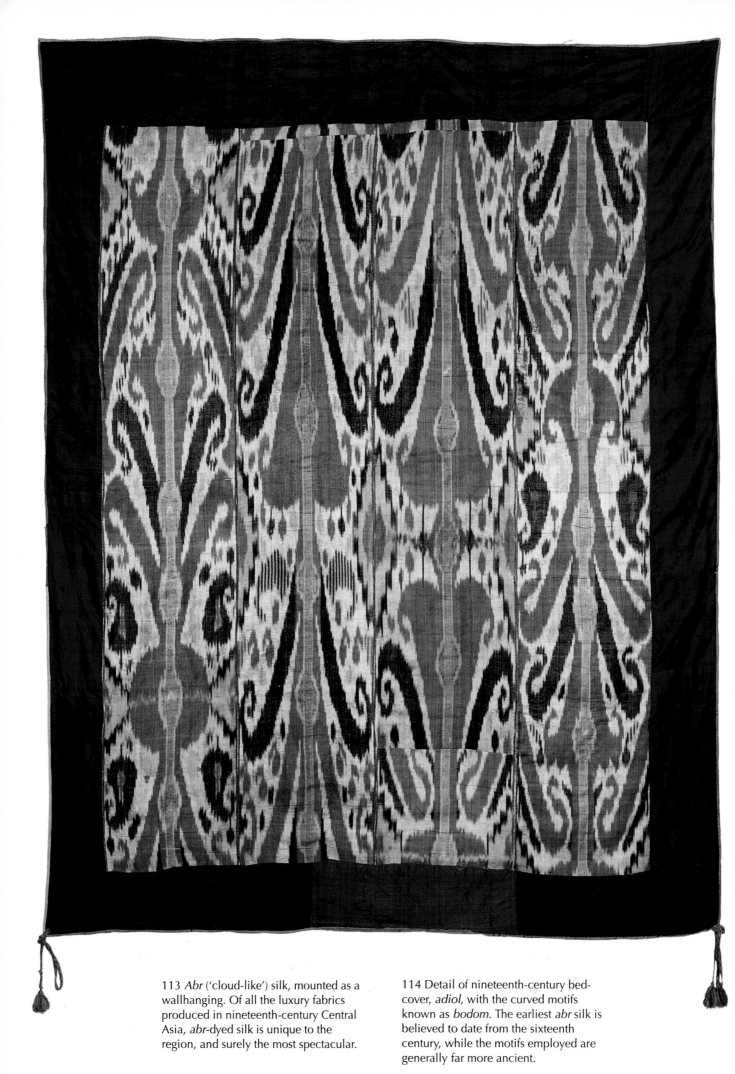

113 *Abr* ('cloud-like') silk, mounted as a wallhanging. Of all the luxury fabrics produced in nineteenth-century Central Asia, *abr*-dyed silk is unique to the region, and surely the most spectacular.

114 Detail of nineteenth-century bed-cover, *adiol*, with the curved motifs known as *bodom*. The earliest *abr* silk is believed to date from the sixteenth century, while the motifs employed are generally far more ancient.

115 (Left) Contemporary brush-dyed *abr,* a popular dress fabric.

116-18 A small number of workshops still produce traditional *abr.* (Above) Marking the silk warps for binding, according to the pattern chosen by the designer. (Right) Binding the warps. (Above right) Threading the manual loom.

119 Nineteenth-century *adras*, ikat-dyed with small *shona gul* ('flower-comb') motifs. The horizontal white lines result from the traditional method of hand-binding the warps.

120 (Right) Nineteenth-century *atlas* (pure silk), ikat-dyed with a pattern of *shona gul* requiring five bindings.

121 (Far left) Machine-printed *faux*-ikat, manufactured in large quantities to meet popular demand throughout the Commonwealth of Independent States.

122 (Left) Wallhanging of a fragment of silk-velvet ikat, *baghmal*, of all nineteenth-century weaves the most costly and exclusive. Involving a complicated double threading of the warp, it was the achievement of many skilled hands in a sequence of workshops.

123-4 (Left and below) *Kurtas*, women's tunics, made of *abr* silk. The *kurta* at left is finished with fine tablet-woven edging-tape, *zeh*. To wear *abr* silk clothing remained an exclusive privilege until the early twentieth century.

125 (Opposite, above) Kirghiz marketwoman in the dark shade of *abr kurta* generally worn by older women.

126 (Opposite, below) Handweaving *abr* silk in a small workshop in the Margellan area.

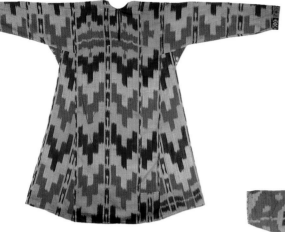

129-30 (Below) Designs with large ram's horn or tambourine motifs were traditional around the oasis towns of Bokhara and Samarkand in the nineteenth century. Complex warp-preparation limited the width of *abr* silk to some 20 cm (12 inches), consequently garments were made with gores or gussets where fullness was required, as for a woman's *chapan* (foot of page).

128 (Above) Man's *abr* silk robe, *chapan*, with the zig-zag pattern known as *kychik*, 'tickling'. Several *chapan* might be worn on top of one another, in a shimmering display of wealth and luxury.

127 (Left) Tadjik family wearing *abr kurtas* and drawstring trousers, typical present-day dress in villages and towns.

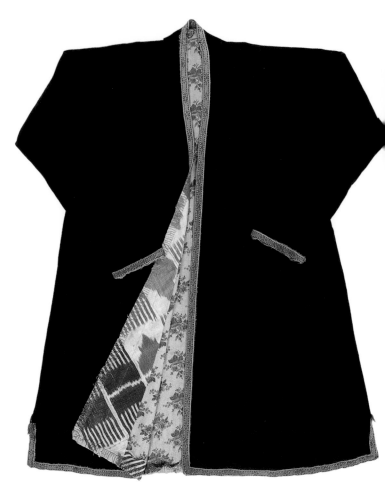

131 Styles varied with the climate and the status of the wearer, but an *abr* silk *chapan* with a padded-cotton lining (above) would have been a fine enough robe for an Uzbek ruler to present to a guest or courtier as the traditional 'robe of honour'.

132 (Above) Nineteenth-century *khalat*, the voluminous robe generally worn by men. This example is finely woven of camel-hair, piece-dyed with indigo. The edging-tape, *zeh*, is made on the garment by an ingenious method of loop-manipulation and needle-weaving.

133 (Left) Silk-brocade *khalat* with *abr* silk lining. The inner edging is embroidered on the coat, while the outer is an attached tape embroidered with cross stitch. *Khalat* were frequently worn draped over the head or shoulders, like a cloak, and many had vestigial sleeves, held together by a band at the back.

134 *Khalat* in the fabric named *mushkar zafar*, 'musk and saffron', woven with dull stripes of blue-black cotton setting off the lustrous stripes of yellow silk. Urban workshops were renowned for their sophisticated use of stripe-widths and textures. This pattern was popular for bridegrooms' robes.

135-6 Religious and social edicts forbidding the wearing of pure silk resulted in the use of silk warps with cotton weft. (Below) Man's *chapan* woven in *bekasab*, a silk-and-cotton mixture with a pronounced diagonal rib. (Below right) Turkmenistan women's gowns made in rich red *adras* (plain-weave) silk-and-cotton. The shawl has an ornate woven border.

137 Hazara woman's velvet gown, adorned with couched gold thread. Though highly esteemed by the Uzbek rulers in the oasis towns, metal-thread embroidery was never denied to the common people, as was silk, and the skill was practised in rural areas.

4 Applied Decoration

Visual stimulation is heightened to the utmost degree of intensity in the decoration of the utilitarian artefacts, clothing and fabrics of the Central Asian nomads. For their part, urban dwellers and the rich élite required elaborate and professionally worked metal-thread embroidery or exquisite silk embroidery on their clothing and the large *suzani* wallhangings and covers. All types of fabric are decorated – leather, felt, wool, cotton and silk – in a variety of techniques, including embroidery stitches applied with a needle or tambour hook, appliqué, painting, stencil, block-print and tie-dye.

Embroidery

Nomad, village and urban traditions

To decorate a plain surface of fabric with embroidery satisfies the creative instinct, and nowhere is this more evident than in Central Asia, where the skill of embroidery is intrinsic to the culture, and the exuberant motifs and colours are as diverse as the ethnic origins of the needlewomen. A woman, be she from a Tadjik, Uzbek, Sart, Turkmen, Khirgiz, Kazakh, Lakai, Hazara or Arab background, whether she lives in a house or a tent, enjoys prestige according to the skill and profusion of her embroideries. A nomad or village girl embroiders from her childhood, learning her skills from her mother and the other women of the family. After her betrothal, traditionally she spends much of her time preparing the dowry textiles for her new home and for the wedding ceremony. In a society in which a woman is valued chiefly as a wife and housekeeper, embroidering brings not only recognition for her skill and industry, but also the pleasure of personal expression and individual creativity. This creativity is evident in the abundance of embroidered surfaces surrounding every-day life. Most functional cloths and clothing are decorated – the hangings that cover the tent or mud walls, or curtain off a sleeping area; cushion-covers, cradle-covers, bed-covers, rugs and bags, especially the small bags that hold personal possessions such as *khol*, used on the eyes, or the *oinakhalta*, to contain a small mirror, or the *chaikhalta*, to carry a supply of tea-leaves, or the small, narrow-necked bag for coins. Animal-trappings are embroidered, as are the traditional women's headdresses and shawls, their bodices and the neck of dresses and tunics, the cuffs of sleeves and trouser-ankles, and of course the hem of the skirt – especially for those garments worn for ceremonies and festivals, where they are displayed for all to see and admire. Many garments are further embellished with amulets, beads, and metal discs, or buttons or zips taken from old western-style clothes sold in the bazaar. A guest will be offered a piece of embroidery as a token of friendship, or as a good-luck talisman for the journey. In their abundance, like flowers in the spring, embroideries bring a lively and colourful extravagance to a way of life that has a high degree of conformity.

Frequently the most beautifully executed embroideries are those made as wedding gifts from the bride to the groom: a belt for his coat or a handkerchief wrapped around love poems, or a beaded triangle, symbol of fertility, to be worn on the little finger of his left hand at the wedding ceremony. A cap for a newborn child, a funerary cover for a relative, a palaquin cover, or the pair of finely embroidered silk 'puttees' wrapped round the bride's hands for the wedding ceremony, will always be stitched with love and care.

Embroidery is solely the craft of women, who thereby preserve the traditional motifs of the tribe. Especially among nomadic pastoralists, these motifs are largely based on the traditional symbols of shamanism and natural forms. The symbols of Islam and 'foreign' art forms are more evident in the designs of urban embroideries. Although there is a strong tribal individuality in the type of stitch used, which to a large extent dictates the style of pattern, whether free-flowing or geometric, many patterns would seem to have changed little over the centuries. Patterns stitched by the Kirghiz and Kazakh today, for example, are similar to those revealed after more than two thousand years of burial at Pazyryk.

All types of thread are used for embroidery – metal thread in urban workshops, wool, cotton, and silk floss. If twisted rather than floss silk is required, the needlewoman does the twisting herself, controlling the tightness of twist and S or Z ply of the thread according to the type of stitch to be worked. She takes fibres from a hank and hooks a bunch around a toe of her outstretched foot, rolling them between the palms of her hands; then plys them by allowing the twisted strands to run together.

Usually one type of stitch dominates the embroidery of a particular tribe or group. A lacing stitch, *kesdi*, is much used by the Turkmen tribes, and satin stitch forms the geometric motifs of the Kohistan embroidery, frequently outlined with white beads. Uzbek and Hazara embroideries are characterized by various types of cross stitch, including the minute stitches which cover the entire fabric to give the surface of intricate geometric patterns typical of their designs. Stem stitch is widely used to outline motifs or form single lines, and a variety of chain stitches, sewn with a needle or tambour hook, form single undulating lines over the fabric or dense, filled-in motifs, as in the large *suzani* hangings. *Basma*, a method of couching a thick thread with a thinner one, is also widely used, especially for metal-thread work and large solid motifs of the *suzani*. Button-hole stitch is common in various forms, and back-stitch for outline.

Some traditional embroidered garments and articles are unique to a specific tribe or area, for example the Turkmen woman's *chyrpy*, the mantle with long vestigial sleeves, worn over the shoulders or the head. The *chyrpy* varies in colour according to the age of the wearer – those of young women are dark blue or black, women of middle-age wear yellow and a matriarch wears white. The outer cloth is always profusely embroidered with stylized floral designs, among which the tulip predominates. Prior to the 1930s the mantle would be lined with beautiful block-printed cotton, but more recently the lining is made of Russian factory-printed cotton.

Silk-thread chain-stitch embroidery decorating a saddle-cover found in the Pazyryk tombs, fourth century BC.

Uzbek cross-stitch embroidery.

Small bag-face worked in ladder-stitch, a Pashtun nomad design of square hooked motifs and embroidered circles holding *shisha* mirrors.

'Flowering-bush' motifs worked in *basma* couching.

The mountain Tadjik of the area around Dushambe make an exquisite wedding veil, *ruband*, which covers the head, face and upper body. It is embroidered in floss silk in a variety of reds, usually on a white background, with motifs of flowers and peacocks which represent the bride and groom. The style is reminiscent of Indian Moghul motifs, and the satin stitch is like that of the Kohistan villages to the south.

Some embroideries of the Lakai are unique in style, their primitive, dynamic, asymmetrical motifs seeming to float on the background fabric. The designs have the archaic appearance of the 'Animal Style' of ancient nomad art. Not contrived, nor with urban influence, they are free-flowing and vibrant with energy, quite unlike the embroideries of other Uzbek groups living in the nomadic tradition, whose cross-stitch embroidery forms a surface of geometric designs. The Lakai decorate bags, tent-hangings, and *saye gosha*, the V-shaped embroideries laid over rolled-up bed-quilts stacked around the tent. Many of these pieces, be they functional or purely decorative, are finished with crochet or a fringe of twisted silk.

The settled Uzbek, Tadjik and Sart people apply embroidery to a range of ceremonial objects. Most notable are *bolim posh*, canopies richly embroidered with symbolic motifs of fertility and fortune, held over the bride and groom during the wedding ceremony. Smaller squares embroidered for the dowry are *lali-posh*, covers for the gifts of sweets, halva, or the even number of *nan*, unleavened bread loaves, which are traditionally offered by the bride's family to that of the groom. The house like the tent is abundantly decorated with embroidered textiles. Long bands known as *zardervori* hang on the walls; *takhai-pos*, embroidered pillow-covers, are piled up on the bedding-chest. Pillow-covers and squares used over a wide area of Uzbekistan, Kazakhstan, Kirghizia and Tadjikistan are decorated with patchwork, *yurok-yastik*. A

Suzani border of floral designs worked in *basma* couching, outlined with chain stitch.

Kesdi-stitch embroidery on a Turkmen *chyrpy*.

Uzbek embroideress working on a *suzani*.

charming domestic embroidered article is the *sandalik posh*, which like the woven *rukorssi* makes a cover for the felts and quilts put over the charcoal brazier. Traditionally the *sandalik posh* of Urgut near Samarkand were embellished with embroidered tea-pots. An important textile made for a girl's dowry is the *ruidigo*. Exquisitely embroidered with floral framing-designs around a central unadorned field, *ruidigo* have a traditional role in marriage custom as a bed-sheet on the nuptial bed.

Suzani, the embroideries used as large hangings, curtains to separate the sleeping-alcove, and covers, are made in the broad area which today comprises Uzbekistan, particularly around the towns of Bokhara, Samarkand, Shakrisyabz, Nurata, Tashkent and Pskent. Those made in the east of the area show the influence of Kirghiz and nomadic Uzbek designs in their large 'moon' discs, *oi palaik*, while those from the western part reflect the style of a settled tradition in their floral designs. The classic hangings, known as 'Bokhara work', embroidered with flowers and meandering vines to adorn the homes of merchants and aristocracy, were usually commissioned from

117

women-embroiderers of the surrounding villages, such as Chafrikan and Gizhduban. In Ferghana a portion of embroidery was left unfinished to allow any trapped *shaitan* (spirits) to make their escape. *Suzani* were also traditionally embroidered by the women of the family for a girl's dowry. The design would be drawn out on four to six narrow woven strips of cotton, *karbos*, by the *kalamkash*, the local designer. Each strip was given to a different embroiderer in the family, and then the finished strips were stitched together. This accounts for the slight misalignment of design often seen in these large embroideries.

Metal-thread embroidery, *zardosi*, was organized in workshop production during the period of the Uzbek rulers, particularly in Bokhara, where areas of the city were given over to the guild-workers who embellished the textiles of the Emir's household. The embroiderers were men, as there was a superstition that women blackened the metal thread. Worked on a frame, the metal thread was couched on to background-fabric of fine wool, cotton, silk or velvet, in elaborate designs. If the embroidery completely covered the fabric the work was known as *zaminduzi*, or if single motifs were scattered across it, *gulduzi*.

Embroidered articles particularly made for Muslim worship are the *djoinamoz*. Used as a prayer mat, and hung on the wall or in a small niche, they have the traditional *mihrab* embroidered in singles or multiples and combined with motifs from pre-Islamic belief, such as pomegranates, tulips and spirals. Small squares of cloth embellished with Islamic symbols are used to wrap prayer-stones. Felt, wool, cotton or

Factory-workers in the common room, with *suzani*-hangings to furnish the walls.

silk squares, with the four corners folded to the centre to make a bag, are richly embroidered to carry the Koran.

Skull caps offer a small field for embroidery, but so various are they in styles of cut, embroidery-stitch and pattern that they could justify a chapter to themselves. Tribes and peoples of a particular area or religion may be identified by their type of skull cap. The cut-out panels which form the cap-shapes are stitched together and embroidered to cover every part of the surface. Cross-stitch forms the all-over patterns of the Uzbek and Hazara caps, while the Tadjik emblazon flower motifs in satin stitch. The caps are made and embroidered by women, and are the one embroidered article that it is acceptable for women to sell in the bazaar, where there is a special section dedicated to them.

A white cock's-comb motif, embroidered on a black skull cap (above) and double-headed bird design worked on a cushion-cover (below).

Block-printing and fabric painting

Printing with carved wooden blocks developed early in the civilization of China, initially to print writing on vegetable-fibre paper. The technique was used to reproduce writing and images by the Buddhist culture which became established around the Tarim Basin, hence the oasis towns of Eastern Turkmenistan have a long tradition of block-printing on paper and cloth. Frequently paper-printing and fabric-printing were carried on in the same premises. The knowledge of block-printing travelled along the trade routes to the towns and villages of Uzbekistan, where a thriving industry of decorative block-printing of cotton developed. The printed cloth provided every-day items such as shawls and wraps, hangings, covers and prayer-cloths, or it was used for dressmaking and for linings for coats and covers.

Ornamentation, mainly naturalistic floral forms, appears not to have changed significantly over a very long period. Motifs on a fragment discovered in the tomb of Timur's wife, Bibi-hanuym, dating from the fourteenth century, and contemporary patterns are very similar.

While Ferghana and Tashkent were well known for printed lengths, Bokhara and the surrounding villages of Dzhondor, Chitgaron and Rometan were famed for the artistic quality of the piece-cloths used for hangings, and bed- and cushion-covers. For a rectangular cover, a popular composition was a large central *oi* (moon) rosette surrounded by detailed floral infilling, bordered by several rows of floral or geometric patterns which complemented or repeated the middle-field decoration. The whole composition formed a well-developed and unified design.

The majority of printing was done on cotton, *karbos*. The soft, fleecy texture of the coarser hand-spun cotton was popular for household textiles, and inspired the contemporary production of printed flannelette covers, now very popular throughout the area.

Typically block-printing was done in two colours, black and red, with the creamy cotton background forming an integral part of the design. The blocks for the motifs' black outlines, known as *basma* (seal), were carved of well-seasoned pear wood, prepared by boiling in mutton fat and cut across the grain of the wood. The fine deep carving and perfectly finished wood made the blocks themselves works of art. Sadly, nowadays the craft of carving wood-blocks has practically died out in Central Asia. The blocks used for the red infilling were rougher, and were carved of a soft wood such as poplar.

Men, *chitagars*, are the printers. The workshop-owner, a highly respected craftsman, designs the pattern for the fabric. He has a set of ready-carved blocks, *kolybs*, and uses his artistic skill to create original compositions. Usually he works with three or four apprentices. The cloth is prepared by soaking in a tannin mordant made from the galls of the pistachio tree, then it is stretched over a low, padded printing-table. A gum of

Block-printing workshop at Margellan in the Ferghana Valley.

iron-solution, stiffened with the resin from apricot trees, or else with flour-paste, is mixed in an earthenware basin and covered with a wool cloth. The block is charged with the liquid by passing it lightly over the wool, and then it is pressed manually on the cotton fabric and given a tap with a wooden hammer. The iron immediately develops as black dye on the tannin-mordanted cloth. After the printing of the black outline-patterns has dried, alum mordant, mixed in a gum with a yellow dye, *tukhmak*, is similarly applied with the second set of blocks, *dud*. After soaking in a madder dye-bath, the cloth takes on an orange-red colour where it is mordanted. The cloth is then well washed and hung in the sun to bleach out any dye from areas not treated with alum mordant.

In some areas an indigo-blue background was achieved by using blocks to apply a mud or flour dye-resisting paste over the black and red patterns, then immersing the whole piece in a vat of indigo dye before washing it well. Cloth dyed in this way was keenly sought after, and commanded a high price, but went out of production in the nineteenth century.

In Bokhara the Jewish indigo-dyers produced silk scarves patterned with block-printed resist motifs, or with small tie-dye dots, and these were available throughout the oasis towns.

Finally, on a small scale and locally, fabrics were also decorated by painting, or with stencil motifs, the most notable example being the hunting cloths produced around Herat, in Afghanistan.

Central Asian printed cloth was renowned for quality and the artistry of its designs, and formed a major export to Russia, until during the nineteenth century the industrialization of the Russian textile industry caused the flooding of the Central Asian markets with cheaper machine-printed fabrics. By the middle of the twentieth century the hand-block-printers of cloth sold from the bolt in the oasis towns had been driven out of business. This, and the introduction of synthetic dyes that were not fast to washing or light, resulted in a general deterioration in quality. Fortunately there were exceptions in the piece-cloths decorated by hand-block-printing, *dostarkhans,* used as hangings, covers and tablecloths. Demand for these has continued, and they have improved to their former high standard since the introduction of the colour-fast alizarin red dye.

138 Nineteenth-century prayer mat, *djoinamoz*, detail. The border design in fine chain stitch is very similar to that of a fragment found in the Pazyryk tombs, dating from the fourth century BC.

139 Couching stitch (*basma*) worked in silk thread on cotton for a *bolim posh*, the canopy held over the bride and groom at the wedding ceremony, from the Urgut area of eastern Uzbekistan, near Samarkand.

140 *Bolim posh* embroidered with
stylized floral discs in *basma* couching.
The dynamic designs with sun discs and
flowers suggest the influence of the
ancient Scythian forms. From the Urgut
area of eastern Uzbekistan, near
Samarkand.

141 (Facing page, far left) Detail of archway-hanging for a Kirghiz tent or house, with the bunched-flower pattern typical of the eastern region of Central Asia.

142 *Suzani* were greatly favoured in Uzbekistan during the affluent period of the Khanates. (Left, above) Dense tambour outlined with chain stitch, detail of an exquisite nineteenth-century hanging from Shakrisyabz. The pattern of flowers and meandering vines is classic 'Bokhara work'.

143 (Left, below) *Suzani* cover from Samarkand, detail. The 'flowering bush' motif in *basma*

couching derives from early Persian decoration, and was popular with the Moghul rulers of India.

144 (Above) Moon-discs, *oi palaik*, on a *suzani*. Embroideries of Tajikistan, Kirghizia and eastern Uzbekistan all prominently display the moon motif. The slight mismatches visible in the pattern show where the portions embroidered by the different women of a family were joined.

145 (Right) Detail of the border of a *suzani* wallhanging, exquisitely worked in *basma* silk couching on fine linen, an example of early nineteenth-century 'Bokhara work'.

146 (Above) *Lali posh*, 'food-cover', embroidered by the women of the bridegroom's family for the gift of halva or flat bread-loaves traditionally offered to the bride's family at the wedding or betrothal.

147 (Left) Kazakh tent-interior with stored textiles.

148-50 (Top and above) *Lali posh*, 'food-covers', embellished with the characteristic patterns of the Lakai and Uzbek. These small ceremonial covers are used by the Uzbek, the Turkmen, and many subtribes.

151 (Above) *Sandalik posh*, the cover for the frame set over the sunken brazier that heats the room. Covers from Urgut, near Samarkand, are traditionally embroidered with small tea-pots.

152-3 (Far left) Small Kirghiz bags, freely embroidered with traditional designs.

154 (Left) *Takhai pos*, cushion- or pillow-cover from Kohistan. All-over geometric patterns are worked with silk-floss satin-stitch in the traditional colours of scarlet and pink.

155 (Opposite) Hazara silk cushion-cover. Extremely fine chain stitch forms the swirling design, and the twisted-silk fringe is edged with blue beads.

156 (Top) Cradle-cloth, *gavara posh*, made to swing hammock-like from a wooden frame or the tent-roof struts. A Kirghiz wool cloth is embroidered in chain stitch.

157-8 (Above) Kirghiz embroidered cover (left) and bag (right), joyously naive in their decorations of finely worked chain stitch.

159 (Facing page) Uzbek satin-weave cotton *gavara posh*, embroidered with *basma* couching outlined in chain stitch, from Samarkand.

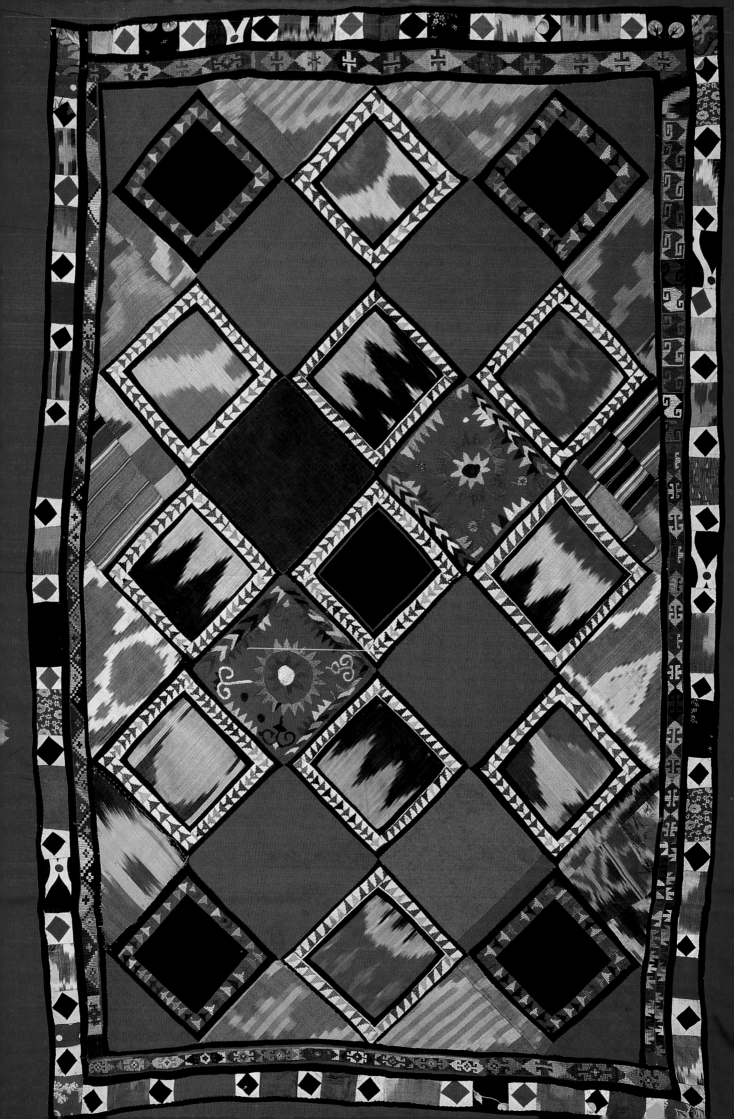

160 *Yuruk yastik*, patchwork, a serviceable fabric made with reclaimed *abr* silk, cotton and embroidery scraps, finished with bands of cross stitch.

161 Tadjik cover combining structured geometric motifs in satin stitch with freely embroidered naturalistic forms, a variety reflecting the different cultural influences that mingle in the towns and villages.

162 The people of the mountainous area of Kohistan – known as Kafiristan, the land of unbelievers, before the conversion to Islam – maintained their animistic beliefs until the late nineteenth century. The motifs of sun discs and trees of life are still prominent in their embroideries. A Kohistani woman's shawl (left) is typically worked with these motifs in red silk-floss satin-stitch on black homespun cotton.

163-4 (Top right) Kohistani tunics, varying in style according to the area. The most elaborate have widely gored skirts and bodices heavy with coins, discs, pearl buttons and old zip-parts.

165 (Far right) Kohistani child's hat, splendidly embroidered with a tree of life outlined in white beads. The back panel is worked as a separate piece.

166 (Below right) Man's coat worked with the typical floral patterns of the mountain villages of Tajikistan. Wool cloth is used for warmth.

167 Uzbek woman's embroidered boots, hand-made with soft leather in the bazaar, and worn on special occasions by the well-to-do.

168-9 (Left and facing page) *Chyrpys*, Tekke Turkmen women's gowns, often lavishly embroidered with small motifs in silk-thread *kesdi* lacing stitch. They are worn over the *kurta* (tunic), cloak-like, covering the head and shoulders, with the long vestigial sleeves hanging down the back and joined by an embroidered band. A dark-coloured *chyrpy* would be worn by a young woman, yellow by a married woman of middle age, and white by a matriarch. The motifs most frequently used are stylized flowers, and especially the tulip, the region's most prolific wildflower.

170 *Saye gosha*, V-shaped embroideries, designed to hang over the rolled-up bed-quilts in tents and houses during the day. *Saye gosha* are used by the many Turkic tribes and display their characteristic motifs and patterns. They also show the high value set on embroidery, and the tribeswomen's pleasure in embellishing their homes.

171 Lakai mirror-bag, *oinakhalta*. The
decoration of silk-strand chain stitch
embroidery on felted wool fabric shows
the freedom and movement of the
hooked motifs of the tribe.

172-3 Many different types of small bag are essential in the Central Asian way of life. They are worn attached to the garments, or hung in a special place in the house or tent. (Above) Tiny circular bags are worked with metal thread, beads and *shisha* mirrors to contain powdered kohl, the eye-cosmetic.

174 (Right) Purses for coins have a long narrow neck which folds over and is secured by a cord. This example is decorated with silk fringes into which blue beads are twisted.

175, 177 (Above and right) Bags are made of two embroidered squares, seamed around three sides and with a drawstring top opening, to hold domestic items such as tea-leaves, or a personal mirror, or embroidery threads. A Central Asian woman, whether Tadjik, Uzbek, Sart, Turkmen, Kirghiz, Kazakh, Lakai, Hazara or Arab, enjoys prestige according to the skill and profusion of her embroideries. Exquisitely embroidered small bags like these are often offered to guests as a memento of the family or a talisman for the ongoing journey.

176 (Above right) Long-necked purse for coins.

178-86 The faces of small bags offer the opportunity for embroidresses to express their creativity in unique miniature masterpieces. Although there are tribal and regional traditions in pattern and type of stitch, the surfaces are generally completely covered with embroidery. Tightly worked interlaced *kesdi* forms the overall geometric design of two Uzbek bags from northern Afghanistan (top left and centre page), while two further Uzbek bags (top right and centre right) are worked in all-over cross stitch.

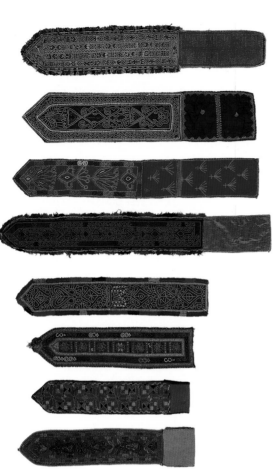

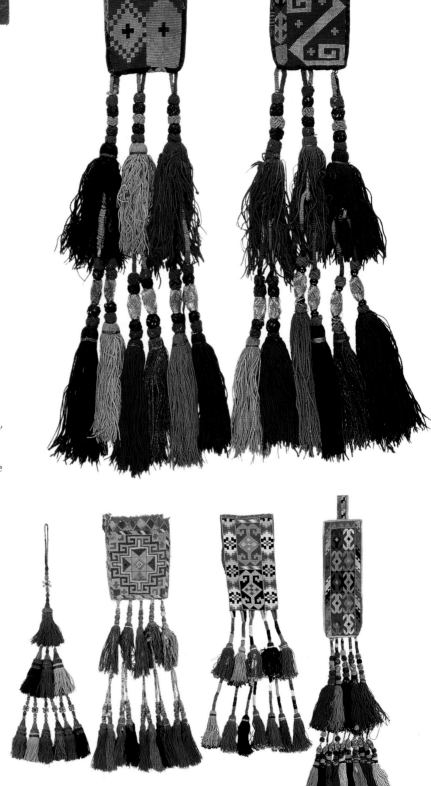

187 (Above) Puttees. The most exquisite embroidery is lavished on bands that are made in pairs by the women of the family, to be wrapped round a bride's hands and wrists for the wedding ceremony. The two shortest bands shown would wrap the bridegroom's wrists.

188-9 (Right and below right) Uzbek decorations for the house or tent, magnificently worked with all-over cross stitch in silk thread. Silk makes elaborate tassels and wrapped cords, decorated with crown knots and metal beads.

190 (Below) Cords with beads and tassels, to be woven into a woman's long plait of hair.

191 Hazara man's shirt-panel. Typical of the
Hazarajat area is white silk-thread embroidery on
white cotton. Here the pattern is formed by the finest
of fine herringbone- and over-stitches, highlighted
with small spots of buttonhole stitch, some red.

192 (Above) Nomad girl's chain-stitch embroidered
dress-front, charmingly naive in design, but skilfully
executed.

193-4 Embroidered squares can be made up into a dress-bodice, or be used with the four corners folded to the centre as a small envelope-bag. Pashtun nomad tribeswomen of Hazarajat have formed these striking symmetrical unit-designs in very closely worked ladder-stitch, finished with woven metal-thread braid and blue beads.

195-9 Stitch-type dictates the style of pattern. Cross stitch or satin stitch are structured on the grid of the fabric, whereas chain or herringbone-stitch can be freely applied. As a general rule one type of stitch is dominant in the embroideries of a village-group, tribe or area, though occasionally the designs are accented with a contrast stitch. While the Uzbek belts (top and above) are worked in all-over cross stitch, the three bag-faces from different regions of Hazarajat (centre) are each worked in a combination of satin stitch and chain stitch.

200-1 (Below) Tightly worked chain stitch giving free linear designs on two bags from Hazarajat.

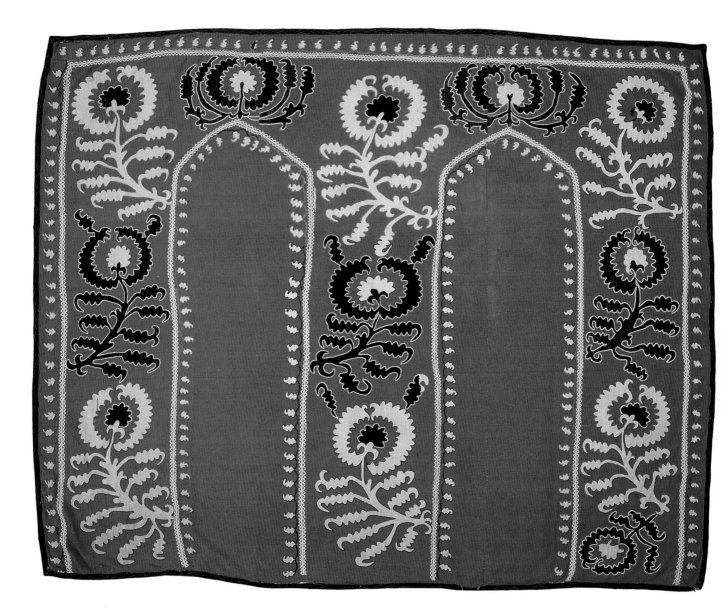

202-3 A small but fertile field for embroidery is offered by skull caps. (Facing page, top and below) Embroidered skull caps worn by men of the Bokharan Jewish community.

204 (Facing page, centre) *Djoinamoz*, prayer cloth from the Sahr-i-Sabz district, with a double *mihrab*. The naturalistic designs are worked in black and white silk thread *basma* couching, each motif outlined in chain stitch in the contrast colour.

205 (Right) Muslim's skull caps, worn wrapped under a long turban by men, and beneath a shawl or veil by women. Designs and embroidery stitches identify the status and origin of the wearer.

206 (Below) Skull cap with a cockerel's-comb motif, a design worn extensively in the oasis towns.

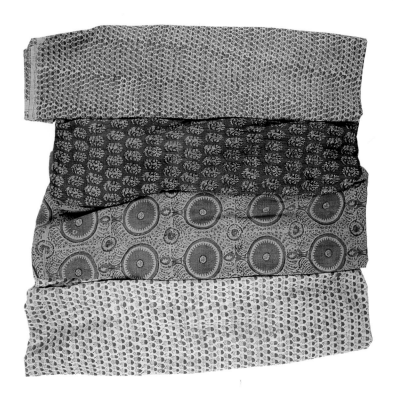

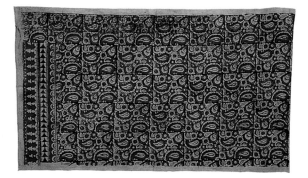

207-8 (Above) Hand block-printed
piece-cloths from Bokhara and the
surrounding villages, designed as a
prayer cloth (top) and bed-cover (detail,
below).

209 (Above right) Block-printed lengths
from the Ferghana area, used for dress
fabrics and robe linings. Patterns are
generally small repeats, since a small
size of printing block is best suited to the
manual technique.

210 (Right) Block-printed piece-cloth,
designed as a bed-cover in the Bokhara
area. The designs of the nineteenth-
century block-prints are generally based
on naturalistic floral forms.

211 Lining of *chyrpy*. The pattern is formed by the application of mud or flour-paste with printing-blocks to resist the indigo dye, a technique that went out of use towards the end of the nineteenth century.

212 (Following page) Roller-printed velvet showing contemporary versions of traditional motifs.

Glossary

Research on the textiles of the area of Central Asia until recently under the administration of the USSR is recorded in the Russian language. Here I have relied on the excellent translations by Sergai Mouraviev. The initial documentation, however, is to be found in the many different languages and dialects in use in the region. To standardize the names of Central Asian artefacts, techniques and tools described in this book I have used the Russian or Persian name except as otherwise indicated in the glossary entries below.

ABR (Persian, literally: 'cloud' or 'cloud-like'). Fabric patterned by binding the warp threads to resist the dye prior to weaving, repeated with several colours. Also known by the Indonesian term 'ikat'.

ABRBAN Craftsman who binds the warp bundles to resist the dye for *abr* (or ikat) weaving.

ADIOL Bed-cover padded with cotton and quilted, used throughout Central Asia.

ADRAS Woven warp-faced fabric with silk warp and cotton weft.

AI KOCHET (Kirghiz) Moon motif.

ALACHA Fine cotton striped fabric.

ALOIZI Variety of silkworm.

APPLIQUÉ Decoration by layering and stitching cut-out motifs or contrast fabrics.

ASMALYK Twin flank-trappings for camel, made of felt or woven, and decorated with embroidery.

ATLAS (Arabic) Satin-weave fabric of silk warp and weft.

AYATLYK (Turkmen) Funerary rug.

BACTRIA Former kingdom which declined in the sixth century AD, comprising the area north of the Amu Darya (River Oxus), extending through northern Afghanistan.

BAGHMAL (Tadjik and Uzbek) Ikat-dyed silk velvet.

BALDACHIN Silk brocade.

BALOUCH Nomadic pastoralist tribes who live north and south of the Amu Darya (River Oxus). Also the belt of desert stretching from eastern Iran through southern Afghanistan and Pakistan.

BAS'CHIRA Persian dialect (Sart) name for Bokhara. *See* 'Beshir ' weavings.

BASKUR (Kirghiz, Karakalpack, Uzbek) Woven band used to tension the nomad trellis-tent (*yurt*).

BASMA (literally: 'seal') Black outline of the patterns printed with wooden blocks. Also couching embroidery stitch; motifs of solid couching are frequently outlined with contrast chain stitch, termed *basma*.

BAST Textile fibre obtained from the stems of plants such as flax, hemp and nettle.

BEATER Heavy pronged hand-tool of wood or metal, or a swinging frame attached to the loom, used to beat-in the weft.

BEKASAB Twill-woven fabric with silk warp and thick cotton weft.

BESHIR Weavings of Ersari Turkmen, named for the town of Bokhara, Bas'chira in the Sart dialect.

BLOCK-PRINT Fabric patterned by motifs applied with carved wood blocks.

BOLIM POSH Canopy held over the bride and groom during the wedding ceremony.

BURKA Cloak of felt or woven wool cloth.

BUTTON-HOLE STITCH Embroidery stitch used to strengthen an edge of fabric, for example round a button-hole.

BUYNUZ (Turkmen) Horn motif.

CARDING The drawing of bunches of fibres through prongs to form them into an orderly roll preparatory to spinning.

CHAIKHALTA Bag to carry tea-leaves.

CHAIN STITCH Linked, looped embroidery stitches forming lines. They can be applied either by needle or hook (tambour).

CHALA MUSLIM Jew converted to the Muslim faith.

CHALMA Cotton turban.

CHAPAN Man's or woman's coat of quilted cotton.

CHARKH Spinning-wheel.

CHARKHTOB Operator of the wheel of the twisting system by which silk thread is formed from a number of reeled silk filaments.

CHASMI BULDUL (literally: 'nightingale's eyes') Indigo and white checked cotton fabric.

CHAVADAN (Kirghiz) Woven bag used to store and carry domestic goods.

CHIRIK Cotton gin, the wooden implement with rollers used to separate the husks from the cotton fibres.

CHITAGAR Block-printer.

CHOWDERI Muslim woman's veil.

CHUVAL (Turkmen) Woven bag used to store and transport domestic goods.

CHYRPY Turkmen woman's embroidered robe with long false sleeves.

CORAL KNOT STITCH Embroidery stitch forming single 'dots'.

COUNTER-SHED Alternative shed of a warp setting.

CROWN KNOT Circular knot of cord or rope.

DAIRA GUL Tambourine motif.

DENIER Unit of weight by which the fineness of silk yarn is measured ($8^{1}/_{2}$ troy grains, fixed in 1839).

DESLIK Collar for the lead-camel of a wedding procession, woven for the dowry and later hung over the tent-door.

DEVCHARKH Large wheel used

to operate the twisting system that forms silk thread from a number of reeled silk filaments.

DJOINAMOZ Embroidered or printed cotton hanging with a central arch or *mihrab* in the design, a prayer cloth.

DORII Fine silk shawl.

DOROI Expecially fine woven silk.

DOSTARKHAN Piece-cloth tablecloth, decorated with block-printing.

DRAWLOOM Handloom with mechanism of cards to lift individual warps for the passage of the weft, allowing the weaving of complicated repeat patterns.

DSCHULCHIR (literally: 'bearskin') Woven long-pile rugs made by the Uzbek.

DUD Carved wood printing-block used to colour-infill black outline patterns.

DUMBA Breed of fat-tail sheep indigenous to Central Asia.

ENSI (Turkmen) Tent-door hanging.

ERSARI Turkmen tribe.

ESHIK TYSH (Kirghiz) Tent-door hanging.

FATIMA Mohammed's daughter. The hand of Fatima is a motif used in Muslim decoration.

FELT Non-woven fabric formed by matting together wool-fibres.

FLAT WEAVE Weaving without pile.

FLOATING WEFT Weft which crosses several warp threads between binding points.

FLOSS SILK Untwisted silk filaments, used for embroidery.

FUGITIVE DYE Colour not fast to light or washing.

FULLING The process of thickening and condensing woven cloth by controlled shrinking.

FUTA A length of cotton fabric worn wrapped round the waist.

FUTABOF Cotton-turban maker.

GAVARA POSH Cradle-cloth.

GERMETCH (Turkmen) Tent-threshold rug.

GHIORDES KNOT Knot used in knotted-pile weave. It is tied on two warp threads, with the ends surfacing between them.

GHUDJERI Rug or cover made of joined strips of warp-face weave.

GLOSSING Treatment applied to woven cotton and silk, using beaten egg-whites and pressure, to give the cloth a stiff, glazed, moiré finish.

GÔL (Turkmen) Tribal emblem in medallion form, woven in carpets, tent-bands and bags.

GUL (Turkmen) Flower motif.

GUL-I-PERON (literally: 'dress flowers') Discs of felt embellished with beads, embroidery and shells, sewn on to garments, bags and animal-trappings as decoration.

GULDUZI (Turkmen) Metal-thread embroidery of single motifs.

GUZA Name for cotton in Western Turkestan.

HAN Chinese dynasty ruling from the second century BC to the third century AD.

HATCHLU (Turkmen) Tent-door hanging.

HAZARA Tribe of Mongolian descent, now living in Central Afghanistan.

HEDDLE Looped threads, held on rods, through which the warp-ends are passed. As the rods are raised or lowered a shed is formed to allow the passage of the weft, according to the pattern.

HSIUNG-NU Aggressive mounted nomadic tribe inhabiting Mongolia prior to the last centuries BC.

IKAT (Indonesian) Fabric patterned by binding the warp threads to resist dye prior to weaving. Also termed *abr* (Persian, 'cloud' or 'cloud-like'). The process of patterning by resist-dying the warps.

IOLAM (Turkmen) Woven band used to tension the nomad trellis-tent (*yurt*).

ISHTIBAR Supervisor of the ikat-weaving workshop.

JALLAR (Turkmen), **JUVAL** (Hazara) Woven bag used to store and carry domestic goods.

KALAMKASH Designer of *suzani*, the large embroideries used as covers or hangings.

KALMI Woven cotton fabric patterned with finely spaced stripes.

KAMONI PAKHTASHAPI 'Bow' used to fluff-up cotton fibres to make padding.

KANAUS All-silk plain-weave fabric.

KAPUNUK (Turkmen) Woven tent-door surround.

KARACHUP Steppeland plant, the source of tannin mordant.

KARAKALPAK Tribe of Mongol descent established on the Altai steppe.

KARAQUL Sheep breed, especially farmed by the Turkmen.

KARBOS Coarse cotton cloth woven with hand-spun yarn.

KARSHIN (Karakalpak) Woven bag used to store and carry domestic goods.

KAZAKH Tribe of Mongol descent established on the northern steppe.

KELIM Weaving technique in which the weft does not travel the full width of the warp, but returns to give adjacent blocks of different colours. Also, a rug woven in flat-weave techniques. Also, the local name for a large main carpet.

KEP General name for a bag throughout Central Asia.

KESDI Embroidery lacing stitch, similar to feather stitch.

KHALAT Man's long-sleeved, loose, thin overcoat of silk or cotton.

KHAN ATLAS All-silk satin-weave *abr* (ikat) fabric. See also *abr*, ikat.

KHIWAZ Name for cotton in Khotan.

KHOSA Bleached fine-cotton cloth.

KHUM Large clay vessel to contain the indigo for cold-dyeing, performed in the dye workshop.

KHURJIN (Uzbek) Pannier-bags.

KIRGHIZ Tribe of Mongol descent established in the Pamir region.

KNOTTED PILE Weave in which short threads are wrapped round warp threads and stand above the ground-weave of alternate weft picks.

KOKI Coarse cotton fabric woven from hand-spun cotton which is kept dry, i.e. not moistened, during weaving.

KOLYB Carved wood block used for printing.

KUDUNGGARI Glossing workshop, where woven cotton and silk fabrics are treated with egg-white and pressure is applied to give a glaze and a moiré finish.

KUROK-YASTIK Patchwork.

KURTA Muslim's long tunic.

KUTCH KARAGUL Ram's horn or scroll motif.

KYCHIK (literally: 'tickling') An ikat pattern of zig-zags.

KYS-GILGAM Woven hangings to separate the men's and women's areas of the tent or house. The finest of these were made for the dowry, and were used during the wedding ceremony.

LAKAI Sub-tribe of the Uzbek who did not embrace Islam, and still maintain a life-style of horsemen and brigands.

LALI POSH Cover for gifts of food.

LOLA GUL Tulip motif.

LIVIT Hank of warp threads separated for binding in the dye-resist process (see *abr*, ikat).

MADRACH (Turkmen) Woven bag used to store and carry domestic goods.

MANDALAK Variety of silkworm.

MARIENA Madder plant, a dye-source.

MIHRAB Islamic 'arch' motif.

MOGHUL A Mongol, especially a follower of Babur, the conqueror of India (1483-1530).

MONGOL A person of Mongoloid stock.

MORDANT Mineral or tannic substance which prepares fibre (or cloth) to absorb and retain dye.

MUNISAK Woman's under-tunic.

MUSHKU-ZAFAR (literally: 'musk and saffron') Black and yellow striped fabric.

NAMAKDAN Woven bag with narrow neck, used to carry salt.

NAMAZLYK Prayer rug.

NISHONZAN (literally: 'he who puts the marks') The craftsman who marks the warp threads to indicate the binding to resist the dye, so creating the designs for *abr* or ikat weaves.

NOIN ULA Ancient Altaian burial site.

NUMDAH Felt rug.

OI Moon motif.

OINAKHALTA Mirror-bag.

OJAKBASHI (Turkmen) U-shaped hearth-surround rug.

OKBASH Long pointed bags woven in pairs as covers for the ends of the tent roof-struts when they are to be carried by the pack-animal.

OK GOZI Arrow motif.

PAKHTASAVVAHUNI The beating of cotton bolls with rods to separate the fibres.

PAKHTAI AMERICON Long-fibre American variety of cotton, introduced to Central Asian cultivation in 1880.

PARDAH (Uzbek and Tadjik) Wallhanging.

PARIPASHA (literally: 'fly's wing') Popular design of white and dark-blue striped cotton.

PARTHIA Ancient kingdom of Scythian peoples, situated on the steppe between the Caspian and Aral Seas.

PATIS Cotton muslin fabric.

PAZYRYK Area in the Altai region at which tomb-barrows dating between 520 and 212 BC were excavated by Russian archaeologists in the early twentieth century.

PILLAKASH-KHONA Silk-reeling workshop.

PILTA The outer layers of the silk filament making a cocoon. The outer silk is inferior in quality, and is spun to make embroidery thread.

PIT LOOM Loom-frame built over a pit which accommodates the treadles used to change the shed with the feet, thus leaving the weaver's hands free to operate the weft shuttles.

PLY Two or more spun threads twisted together.

PODSHOKHI (literally: 'emperor's cloth') All-silk plain-weave fabric.

POSHTIN Coat of sheepskin, or a fur-lined silk coat.

RAMIE Bast fibre obtained from an indigenous Central Asian plant.

RANGUBORCHI Hot-dyers.

RAW SILK Silk filament with the natural sericin or gum still present, prior to treatment or twisting.

ROLAG Roll of cotton or wool fibres prepared for spinning.

RUBAND Embroidered wedding-veil of the mountain Tadjik.

RUIDIGO Sheet for the nuptial bed, embroidered for the dowry.

RUKORSSI Felt or woven cover for the *sandik*, the sunken charcoal brazier which heats the room.

RUMOL Silk scarf worn by women in all parts of Central Asia.

RUYAN Madder plant, source of dye.

SAKA Early nomadic tribe of Transoxiana.

SAKSAUL Woody plant which grows underground in desert areas, used as fuel by nomadic peoples.

SALLABOF Makers of silk turbans.

SALLANCHAK Woven hanging-cradle.

SALOR Turkmen tribe.

SALORI BULUR Cotton fabric woven with thick and thin yarns.

SARMATIANS Early nomadic tribe of the central steppelands.

SANDALIK POSH Embroidered cover for the *sandik*, the sunken charcoal brazier which heats the room.

SAR-O-PAR (literally: 'head-to-foot') Term for a set of new clothing formerly given annually to members of the court or household by an Islamic ruling family. The custom continues, but in a small way.

SART Urban Persian-speakers, settled nomadic peoples. Persian dialect.

SARYQ Tribe of Turkmen origin.

SAYE GOSHA (Uzbek) V-shaped embroidered decoration.

SCYTHIANS Early settled peoples

155

who occupied western Central Asia, and developed the 'Animal Style' of art characterized by dynamic motifs of intertwined beasts.

SEHNA KNOT Knot used in knotted-pile weave. It is tied on two warp threads with the pile ends surfacing singly, either to the right or the left of the warps.

SERES Name for the inhibitants of China (Serinda) in the time of the writings of Pliny (AD 41-54)

SERICULTURE Breeding of silkworms to produce silk.

SERINDA Name for ancient China (see Seres).

SHABADAN (Kazakh) Bag used to store and carry domestic goods.

SHABRACK Horse-blanket.

SHAITAN Evil spirit.

SHED Parting of warp threads to permit the passage of the weft.

SHISHA Small pieces of mirror-glass inserted among embroidery.

SHOKI BARGIKARAM (literally: 'silk of cabbage leaves') Design of silk fabric.

SHONA GUL Comb-flower motif.

SILK FLOSS Untwisted silk filaments, used for embroidery.

SINNET Form of knotting, braided cordage.

SOUFREH Woven square or rectangle used to make clean surface for the preparation and eating of food.

SPARAK Indigenous steppeland plant yielding a yellow dye.

SPUN SILK Silk thread spun from inferior quality or broken silk filaments, used for embroidery.

SUBSTANSIVE DYE Natural dye which colours fibres or fabric without use of a mordant.

SUFA Platform, usually of packed mud, e.g. in a dye workshop.

SUMACH Weft-wrap weave.

SUZANI Large embroidered cloth used as a cover or hanging.

TABBY WEAVE Plain weave.

TABLET WEAVING Weaving with the warp ends threaded through holes in wood, bone or card tablets, which are manually rotated to form the shed. The method is used to weave narrow widths, as the number of warp ends that will be threaded through the tablets is limited by the number of tablets which can be conveniently operated by the weaver.

TADJIK People of Persian origin who settled in Central Asia.

TAKHAI-POS Embroidered cushion or pillow-cover.

TEKKE Turkmen tribe.

TING-TINGCHI Operator of the 'bow' used to fluff-up cotton fibres for use as padding.

TOR Place of honour in a nomad trellis tent (yurt), on the wall facing the opening.

TRANSOXIANA Area of steppe between the Oxus and Jaxartes Rivers.

TSENG HUNG HUA (Tibetan red) Red dye obtained from safflower.

TUKHMAK Yellow dye used in block-printing cotton.

TURKIC Of the Turkmen peoples.

TURKMEN Main tribe of Mongoloid descent.

TWILL WEAVE Weave-system based on a unit of three or more ends and three or more picks, in which the binding point moves along by one end at each pick, forming a diagonal line in the weave.

UIGHUR People of Mongolian descent who settled in Eastern Turkestan, and who formulated written Mongolian.

USTO Craft workshop overseer.

UZBEK Followers of Uzbek Khan (1312–40), a descendant of the Mongol ruler Genghis Khan. From the seventeenth century the Uzbek tribe became very powerful in the oasis cities of Bokhara, Samarkand and Ferghana.

WARP Longitudinal threads of a textile, held under tension on a loom.

WEFT Transverse threads of a textile.

WEFT-WRAPPING Weave in which the weft wraps round each of the warp ends in turn. Also termed sumach.

YALANGDAVRON Ikat (resist-dyed) striped cotton. See also abr and ikat.

YOMUD Tribe of Turkmen descent.

YUEH-CHI Mounted nomads of the northern steppelands.

YULDUZ (Kirghiz) Star motif.

YURT (Turkmen; literally: 'home territory'). The common name for the nomads' trellis tent.

ZAMINDUZI Metal-thread embroidery which covers the background fabric.

ZARDERVORI Long embroidered band used as a hanging.

ZARDOSI (Tadjik) Metal-thread embroidery.

ZAR-I-CHOUB (literally: 'yellow wood') Indigenous steppeland plant yielding a yellow dye.

ZEH Patterned-silk edging-tape made by a number of different techniques, including tablet-weaving.

Further Reading

HISTORY OF THE REGION AND ITS TEXTILES
Bussagli, Mario, *Central Asian Painting*, Geneva, 1979.
Hopkirk, Peter, *Foreign Devils on the Silk Road*, Oxford, 1980.
Jackson, W.A. Douglas, *Russo-Chinese Borderlands*, Princeton, NJ, 1962.
Krist, Gustav, *Alone Through the Forbidden Land*, E.O. Lorimer, London, 1937.
Kwanten, Luc, *Imperial Nomads*, Leicester, 1979.
Leix, Alfred, *Turkestan and its Textile Crafts*, The Crosby Press, Basingstoke, 1974.
Lindahl, D. and Knorr, T., *Uzbek*. Exhibition catalogue, The Textile Gallery, London, 1975.
Michaud, Roland and Sabrina, *Caravans to Tartary*, London, 1978.
Muqi, Che, *The Silk Road*, Beijing, 1989.
National Geographic, Vol.177, No.3, *The Golden Hoards of Bactria*, Vikto Ivanovich Sarianidi.
Nomads of Eurasia, Exhibition catalogue, Natural History Museum of Los Angeles County, edited by Vladimir N. Basilov, Seattle, 1989.
Phillips, E.D., *The Royal Hordes – Nomad Peoples of the Steppes*, London, 1965.
Rudenko, Sergai I., *Frozen Tombs of Siberia, The Pazyryk Burials of Iron-Age Horsemen*, trans. M.W. Thompson, London, 1970
Simkin, C.G.F., *Traditional Trade of Asia*, London, 1968.
Stein, Sir Aurel, *On Ancient Central-Asian Tracks*, Chicago, 1974.
Talbot Rice, Tamara, *Ancient Arts of Central Asia*, London, 1965.
Teaque, Ken, *Metal Crafts of Central Asia*, Princes Risborough, 1990.
The Travels of Marco Polo, trans. Ronald Latham, London, 1958.

MOTIFS USED IN TEXTILE DECORATION
Albarn, K., J.M. Smith, S. Steele and P. Walker, *The Language of Pattern*, London, 1974. For Islamic pattern.
Petrie, Flinders, *Decorative Patterns of the Ancient World*, London, 1990.
Talbot Rice, David, *Islamic Art*, London, 1993.

THE MATERIALS AND DYES
Burnham, Dorothy K., *A Textile Terminology*, London, 1980.
Gittinger, Mattiebelle, *Master Dyers to the World*, Washington, DC, 1982.

FELT
Burkett, Mary E., *The Art of the Felt Maker*, Kendal, 1979.

Faegre, Torvald, *Tents, Architecture of the Nomads*, London, 1979.

YARN CONSTRUCTION
Bidder, Hans, *Carpets from Eastern Turkestan*, London, 1964.
Collingwood, P., *The Techniques of Rug Weaving*, London, 1968.
—, *Textile and Weaving Structures*, London, 1987.
The Ersari and their Weavings, Exhibition catalogue, International Hajji Baba Society, Washington, DC, 1975.
Hull, Alastair, Jose Luczyc-Wyhowska, *Kilim, The Complete Guide*, London, 1993.
Ikat, Woven Silks from Central Asia, The Rau Collection, Oxford, 1988.
Kalter, Johannes, *The Arts and Crafts of Turkestan*, London, 1984.
Konieczny, M.G., *Textiles of Baluchistan*, London, 1979.
Loges, Werner, *Turkoman Tribal Rugs*, trans. Raoul Tschebull, London, 1980.
Moshkova, V. G., *Carpets and Rugs of the Peoples of Central Asia*, Moscow, 1970.
Roth, H. Ling, *Studies in Primitive Looms*, Bedford, 1978.
Rugs of the Yomud Tribes, Exhibition catalogue, International Hajji Baba Society, Washington, DC, 1976.
Thompson, Jon, *Carpet Magic*, Barbican Art Gallery, London, 1983.
Tursunov, N.O., *History of the City Handicrafts of Northern Tadzhikistan*. Dushambe, 1974, trans. Sergai Mouraviev, 1993.
Tzareva, Elena, *Rugs and Carpets from Central Asia*, The Russian Collection, Moscow, 1984.

APPLIED DECORATION
Andrews, Mugul and Peter, *Turkmen Needlework*, London, 1978.
Butler, Anne, *The Batsford Encyclopedia of Embroidery Stitches*, London, 1979.
Dupaigne, Bernard, Roland Paiva, *Afghan Embroidery*, Pakistan, 1993.
Paine, Sheila, *Embroidered Textiles, Traditional Patterns from Five Continents*, London, 1990.
Sidorenko, A.I., A.R. Artykov, R.R. Radjabov, *Gold Embroidery of Bokhara*, Tashkent, 1981.
Sukhareva, O.A., *The Folk Decorative Art of Soviet Uzbekistan*, section 'Artistic Cloth Printing', Tashkent, 1954, trans. Sergai Mouraviev, 1993.
Valeeva-Suleimanova, Guzel, and Rozalina Shageeva, *The Decorative Applied Art of the Kazan Tatars*, Moscow, 1990.

Museums and Galleries

During the nineteenth and early twentieth century, at the period when most of the world's renowned museums were gaining collections, Central Asia was closed to travellers. However, over the past few decades many interesting Central Asian textiles have been carried out of the country by refugees and sold in the bazaars of Kabul, Istanbul and Peshawar to foreign collectors and traders. In the West, fine embroideries, weavings, ikats and rugs may be found in specialist shops and galleries. A few major museums hold small collections of Central Asian textiles, usually in store. The most representative and finest displays, however, are to be found in the local ethnology museums of the region.

AFGHANISTAN
Kabul
National Museum of Afghanistan, Darul Aman
Khulm
Khulm Museum, Royal Palace

COMMONWEALTH OF INDEPENDENT STATES

RUSSIA
St Petersburg
State Hermitage Museum
State Museum of Ethnography
Moscow
Russian Federation Museum of Decorative, Applied and Folk Art, Delegatskaya

KAZAKHSTAN
Alma-Ata
Museum of Decorative Arts

TAJIKISTAN
Dushambe
Tadzikskij Istoriceskij Muzej

TURKMENISTAN
Ashkhabad
Turkmenskij Gosudarstvennyj Muzej, Izobrazitel'nych Iskusstu Central'nyj Gosudarstvenny Muzej Turkmenskoj

UZBEKISTAN
Bokhara
Regional Museum

Tashkent
Gosudarstvennyj Muzej Istorii Narodov Uzbekistana (silk production)
Muzej Prikladnogo Iskusstra (textiles)
Gosudarstvennyj Muzej Iskusstra Uzbekistana (handicrafts).

FRANCE
Paris
Musée de l'Homme

PAKISTAN
Peshawar
Peshawar Museum

PEOPLE'S REPUBLIC OF CHINA
Dunhuang
County Museum (for Silk Road relics)

SWITZERLAND
Basle
Museum für Volkerkunde

UNITED KINGDOM
London
Horniman Museum (for felts)
Museum of Mankind
Victoria and Albert Museum
Oxford
Pitt Rivers Museum

WEST GERMANY
Munich
State Ethnological Collection
Stuttgart
Linden Museum

USA
Washington, DC
The Textile Museum

Sources of Illustrations

All studio photography is by James Austin, with the exception of pls. 1, 25-6, 44, 73, 86, 113, 128-9 photographed by Barry Dawson.

Textiles for the colour plates were kindly lent by Janet Anderson 21, 22, 27, 142; Bambi 2; Nicholas Barnard 122; Olivia Bristol 138; Peter and Elizabeth Collingwood 112, 162, 168, 211; Joyce Doel 167; Maria Fields 163, 165; John Gillow 20, 25, 33, 37, 40, 42-3, 45, 55-6, 78, 115, 133, 135-6, 139-41, 143-4, 151, 159, 161, 204; Richard Harris 73, 80, 81, 82; Rupert Harvey 1, 12, 13, 67, 154; Alastair Hull 11, 19, 34, 85-7, 90, 105, 128, 166, 212; Raymond Hull 75, 93; Cynthia Kendzior 145; Pip Rau 5, 23, 32, 35-6, 47-8, 76, 79, 83-4, 114, 119-21, 123-4, 130-1, 148-50, 152-3, 156-8, 169, 175-86, 202-3, 207-10; Karun Thakur 46; the remainder 3, 4, 6, 7, 14-18, 24, 26, 28-31, 38-9, 41, 44, 49-54, 57-65, 66, 69, 72, 74, 77, 88-9, 91-2, 94-104, 106-111, 129, 132, 134, 137, 146, 155, 160, 164, 170-4, 187-9, 201, 205 are from the author's collection.

Location photograph acknowledgements are due to John Gillow pl. 71, 116-8, 126; Joel Gillow pl. 127; Inman Harvey pl. 10, 70; John Pilkington pl. 8, 9, 68, 125, 147, 206.

All line drawings are by Bryan Sentance, with the exception of p. 96 drawn by Tess Recordon. The maps on p. 10-11 and 14 are drawn by Michael Edwards.

Black-and-white photographs are acknowledged to Mary E. Burkett p. 63; Maggie Kemp p. 48, 68, 69, 91; Pitt Rivers Museum, Oxford p. 12, 13, 15, 47, 65, 67; Private collection p. 16, 92, 94, 117, 118, 120; State Hermitage Museum, St Petersburg p. 62, 71; Courtesy of the Board of Trustees of the Victoria and Albert Museum p. 95.

Index